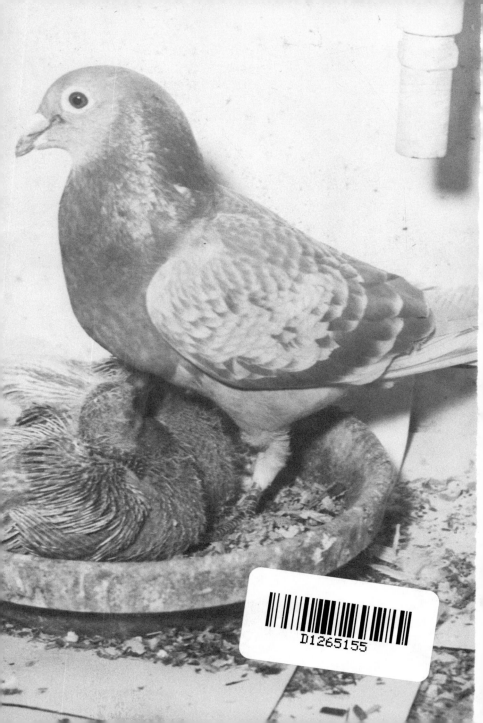

A domestic pigeon with completely white feathers. Domestic breeds when released in the wild will usually disappear after several generations. A CLI photo.

Opposite:
An almost life-like mounted specimen of a Passenger Pigeon *(Ectopistes migratorius)* in a natural setting. This extinct species at one time occupied the eastern half of North America, from Canada to Louisiana and Florida. A San Diego Zoo photo.

Introduction

Pigeons and doves form a very distinct family, with such special characteristics that anyone can tell them from other birds. Especially peculiar is the shape of the bill and feet: the bill is straight and slender, rather weak, horny at the tip only, and soft at the base; the legs (tarsi) are thick and fleshy, and the toes have short, curved nails.

5

The numerous species of pigeons and doves—doves are simply small pigeons—are distributed throughout the world: they are found even on very small islands. They are monogamous, as most of them live in pairs, flocking at certain seasons, while others are gregarious at all times. Pigeons and doves usually nest in trees, building flimsy platforms on twigs; a few, however, nest on ledges, in cliff and tree holes, or on the ground. Their usual clutch consists of two eggs, sometimes of only one. The young are fed by the male and the female, for the first days of their lives, on a milky liquid secreted in the crop of the parents—a very special feature among birds; they are poorly feathered and helpless at birth, and they usually remain in the nest until they are well developed.

Excellent aviary birds, pigeons and doves live long and breed well. Keeping them has the following advantages: they do not damage vegetation and can therefore be housed in planted flights; they do not, as a rule, bother other birds; and they rear their young themselves.

There are two main groups or subfamilies of pigeons: the Seed-eating Pigeons (Columbinae) and the Fruit Pigeons (Treroninae). The latter have very short, fleshy, feathered legs and a soft bill; their plumage is usually bright, with much light green, and gaudy markings of red, pink, yellow, and other vivid colors. These birds are completely arboreal in habits, living in trees, where they feed on fruit and berries. They occur in the Old World only, being most numerous in Malaysia, Australia, and the islands of the Pacific. The Seed-eating Pigeons, found throughout the world, are abundant in the Americas. They have longer, naked legs, harder bills, and eat mostly seeds; a number live and feed on the ground. They seldom show bright colors, but are mostly brown or gray, with elegant markings of black-and-white tones; some show metallic green, blue, and purple markings of great beauty.

All pigeons and doves are handsome birds, elegant in shape and pleasing in color, including even those whose plumage is predominantly brown or gray, as they are always harmoniously blended and often tinged with green, pink or purplish reflections.

Pigeons and doves have long been favorites with a number of amateur aviculturists, but today they are not as popular as perhaps they deserve to be—as are, for example, budgerigars and other parrot-like birds. Many breeders, however, rear the more

Barbary Dove, domesticated form of the African Collared Dove.
Photo by H.V. Lacey.

generally-kept species in large numbers, both in American and
European aviaries, particularly in California, where all species can
be kept outdoors the year round. Several zoological gardens have
good collections, and there are outstanding ones in the aviaries of
J.W. Steinbeck, Concord; Carl Naether, Encino; and in my own at
Cleres, France. More recently a number of excellent private collections are being maintained, mostly on the West Coast, and
there is an American Dove Association. A. Decoux, also in France,
had for many years been successful with rare doves. Before World
War II, the late Mme. E. Lacallier possessed one of the finest
series ever assembled. Those of the late Miss Rosie Alderson,
H.D. Astley, T.H. Newman and A. Ezra, all in England, were
considerable, as was that of Dr. E.W. Gifford in Oakland,
California.

Upper photo:
Masked Dove (*Oena capensis*). The female lacks the white-bordered black marking on the face of the male. Photo courtesy of Vogelpark, Walsrode.
Lower photo:
A Mourning Dove *(Zenaida macroura)* photographed while feeding in an exposed area of the zoo. A San Diego Zoo photo.

Tambourine Dove *(Turtur tympanistria).* This dove is also known by many other names: White-breasted Wood Dove, Forest Dove and White-breasted Pigeon. Photo by P. Kwast.

These Diamond Doves have reared many young in a cage which was previously used as a rabbit hutch. However, they are best kept in an aviary at other times. Photo by H.V. Lacey.

Pigeons and Doves in Captivity

HOUSING

Pigeons and doves are generally flying and perching birds and should be kept in aviaries enclosed with wire netting. Even those species which spend most of the time on the ground, roost up and nest in trees, with very few exceptions. As they require plenty of fresh air and a reasonable amount of exposure to sunlight and to rain, the larger part of a suitable aviary consists of an open-air flight, with a house at the rear, to which they can retreat whenever necessary. Most species, even many tropical ones, prove so extremely hardy that they can be successfully kept outside in winter, with the simple help of an unheated shelter, even in cold countries such as northeastern North America and western Europe. The more delicate species should be kept inside and be given some artificial heat during the winter, but only enough to avoid frost. Even those, however, should be kept outdoors from May to October, as they will neither remain in good plumage nor will they be likely to breed if kept in indoor cages throughout the year. The Ground Pigeons are generally too small to be safely kept pinioned in an unroofed enclosure, but the very large Crown Pigeons or Gouras, the size of big hens, can live in a fenced-in garden. They are sometimes tame enough to be left full-winged; but they are more usually housed in aviaries.

There are two different ways of housing pigeons and doves: in large flights, where several pairs are placed together, or in smaller pens designed for one pair, or sometimes two pairs. In the latter case, they should be sufficiently different in size and habit, so that they do not compete for territory. The most aggressive and bad-tempered species must always be kept in such a way. The number of pairs associated in a large aviary depends upon its size but only

Green-winged Dove *(Chalcophaps indica)*. This is a widely spread species in its range; several subspecies have been described.

Opposite:
On account of noise produced by a large group of pigeons put together in one place an aviary should not be built very near people's houses. In addition, the aviary has to conform with the building codes and zoning laws of a city or town.

one pair of each species should inhabit the same aviary. A range of flights 30 feet long, eight feet wide, eight feet high is very suitable for three or four pairs to live and breed satisfactorily in each compartment. They should be provided on the north end with a shelter built of wood, brick, or concrete that extends the whole width of the pen. The open flight will be more suitable if planted with trees and shrubs and the shelter provided with pine boughs and branches. Perches, one-inch thick, should be nailed on the sides, and shelves fixed against the walls indoors, as doves like to run and rest on them.

The floor of the shelter should be made up of concrete to shut out digging rodents and to afford easy cleaning; also, it should be covered with a mixture of sand and wood ashes, for certain doves never bathe, but, like chickens, dust themselves. The frames of the wire netting panels should either rest on a two-foot-deep concrete foundation, or else be buried two feet in the ground to avoid the intrusion of rats and other digging vermin, which would kill or disturb the birds, particularly the young. The frames can be made of wood or metal. The mesh of the netting should be small: half-inch mesh will keep out sparrows, small rats and large mice, but young ones will be kept out only by quarter-inch mesh. Most of

Floor construction for pigeon flight showing three types of plans for direction of drainage.

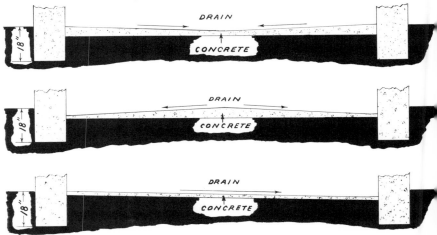

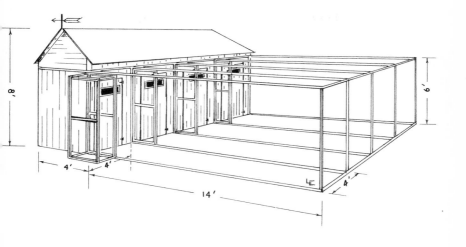

Flight for housing pigeons and doves.

my own dove aviaries have half-inch mesh, and the small mice which get in from time to time can easily be eliminated by keeping a constant supply of Warfarin—an effective rodent poison—under special boxes which the birds cannot enter.

The shelter is made of solid walls on three sides, with only the front opening into the flight. The trap-door of the shelter, if the front is not left completely open, is best placed near the ground, as doves prefer it to a door higher up. There is also a door of solid wood or part-glass to allow one to enter. According to climate and circumstances, the flight may face south, east, or west, and be so situated as to provide shelter from the dominant wind, which doves cannot long endure. It is advisable to fix the wire netting so that it remains flexible, as doves are subject to panics, particularly at night, and may injure their heads as they dash against the partitions. Where hawks are numerous, particularly Cooper Hawks in America, they present a serious problem because they terrorize the doves, which then madly strike the wire-netting and injure

Bronze-winged Pigeon *(Phaps chalcoptera).* Photo by Dr. Herbert R. Axelrod.

Opposite, upper photo:
One of two eggs normally laid by a Bronze-winged Pigeon is partly visible under this nesting bird. Note the brightly colored and iridescent wing feathers. Photo by K. Hindwood.

Opposite, lower photo:
Bronze-winged Pigeons build their nests in trees and shrubs and occasionally in the hollows and ledges of rocks and on the ground. Photo by Dr. Herbert R. Axelrod.

themselves, sometimes dying of broken skulls. In that case, it is necessary to provide ready shelters and thick cover to which they can easily take refuge.

When cats, hawks or other pests are numerous, it is sometimes necessary to have double wire netting roofs and fronts, two or three inches apart; or to cover most of the roof with plastic material. An alternative to a range of pens is a much larger flight, where twenty or more pairs can be settled. Such aviaries should be eighty to 100 feet long and twenty to thirty feet wide, heavily planted, with a roomy shelter along one or two sides. To insure privacy for the breedings pairs, the shelter can be divided into a number of alcoves, two feet wide, by means of vertical boards thirty inches broad running from top to bottom. Such a method was very successfully used by Dr. E.W. Gifford at Oakland, California.

Small compartments, twelve to fifteen feet by four to six feet, generally built much like the larger ones already described, are suitable for one pair of large doves. Another pair of smaller ones may be added if the former belong to a quiet and fairly good-tempered species.

In all cases, other birds can be associated with pigeons and doves, if they are harmless to them, their eggs, and their young. But one must remember that individuals vary in temper; therefore, every case must be watched carefully.

In mild climates, such as those of California, the southern United States, and the Mediterranean countries, where all pigeons and doves can be kept outdoors the year around, the shelter at the rear of the aviary should be left completely open in front. In colder areas, it should be separated from the open flight by a solid partition with windows and doors which can be shut during inclement weather. As we have said before, many species are hardy enough to be kept without artificial heat the year around, if they are given a comfortable, dry, and well-lighted shelter, where they can take refuge during heavy rains and on frosty nights. It may be wise to confine them to the shelter during cold spells, but the majority find the branches of conifers and other evergreen trees adequate protection. Tender species, however, should be kept in a slightly heated shelter, or moved to a warm room during the winter. Most of the ground doves are better treated in this manner, for,

Most doves and pigeons can be housed with smaller birds, such as finches, mynahs, etc., except for a few really very quarrelsome birds. Photob y L. van der Meid.

although they can stand a good deal of cold, their thick, fleshy legs are susceptible to frost bites. This usually does not kill them, but the loss of toes cripples them, thus making them useless for breeding purposes. Since most Fruit Pigeons are susceptible to cold, they should be kept in places free from frost.

When pigeons and doves arrive from their native countries, they require special care. They are timid, rather stupid birds, startled by the least disturbance, and they dash head-first against the bars or the roof of their traveling cage in the most distressing way. Some kill themselves in their panic; others split the skin of their heads and are scalped—disfigured for the rest of their lives. To avoid such accidents, one should pad the roof of the traveling cases and arrange for the bird to get light through oil paper or plastic

Crested Pigeon *(Ocyphaps lophotes)*. This species is found throughout Australia, except in very wet areas of the continent. Photo by A. J. Mobbs.

Opposite:
A Crested Pigeon photographed in captivity at the San Diego Zoo. In the wild
they feed in great numbers; as many as
a thousand in a single spot have been
recorded. Photo by Dr. Herbert R.
Axelrod.

View of an aviary that is enclosed by wire netting. These Blue Ground Doves *(Claravis pretiosa)* are protected from strong wind currents by the trees and bushes growing outside. Photo by L. van der Meid.

cloth without being able to see out, thus avoiding hard wire netting or bars. If they arrive in good condition and in favorable weather, the best thing to do is to turn them out into a small, well-sheltered aviary, provided with plenty of thick trees, boughs, and fine sand; they should be the only occupants of the aviary. They can be kept in the open flight for a few hours, but must be shut up in the shelter in wet or windy weather, and at night. In this way, the birds will soon get used to captivity and become tame; it will then be time to settle them into their permanent aviary and to let them associate with other birds. If they arrive ill or very tired, they must be placed in an inside cage well provided with green boughs among which they can hide. The cage should have a roof of canvas to prevent head injuries, and every precaution should be taken to avoid panics while feeding the doves or cleaning their cages.

Doves should not be kept too long in cages, because they are not suitable for such timid, nervous birds. A few months are usually needed for them to recover sufficiently from their trip.

The legend of the gentleness of doves is, unfortunately, not born out of facts. Aviculturists know that contrarily doves are quarrelsome and jealous, which behavior is to be considered when they must be kept with other birds. The French breeders, the first to be successful in breeding the rarer doves about 1880, when they began to be imported, first isolated each pair in a special compartment. Occasionally, they added a few pheasants, quails or waders to their pens, since such birds, living on the ground, did not come much in contact with them. Further experience showed that these excessive precautions were not necessary. Certain species, such as the Australian Crested, Plumed, Bar-shouldered, and Grayson's, are very pugnacious and must be kept in separate pens, or only with strong birds which they cannot injure, such as pheasants and parrots. Fortunately, evil-tempered species are so few that most of them can be kept together safely and successfully. It is always wise not to put more than one pair of the same or closely-related species into the same pen, although a few will breed in colonies. Admittedly, birds of different temper are found within the same species: one pair may be peaceful, another, quarrelsome. For this reason, they should be watched for the first few weeks after they have been placed with other birds.

We have already said that pigeons and doves can be kept with pheasants, if the latter are not spiteful; they will live also with other birds. The smaller species, such as Diamond, Cape (Masked), Zebra, Pigmy, Passerine, and others do well with various finches and waxbills. Ground pigeons and Bronze-wings may be kept with wydahs, weavers, insectivorous birds, and many other perching birds. Quails do well with doves, except the very quarrelsome varieties, and American quails, such as the California Valley Quail, disturb the doves because they perch and may upset their nests.

Young doves should be removed from the parents' aviary about one month after they have left the nest. If moved too early, they may suffer and die, as they remain very delicate for some weeks. If left longer, they may interfere with the parents' next brood, and be bullied and even killed by them.

The facial markings of the Plumed Dove *(Lophophaps plumifera)* are clearly seen in this photo. Photo courtesy of Vogelpark Walsrode.

Partridge Bronze-winged Pigeon *(Geophaps scripta)*. This pigeon is also called Squatter Pigeon. Some ornithologists place the species in the genus *Petrophassa*. Photo by A.J. Mobbs.

The interior of the aviary can be designed in several ways according to the principal aim of the owner, whether purely utilitarian or rather ornamental. Personal taste and ingenuity come into play; it is usually possible to make the interior both pleasant and practical, if one uses the imagination, as well as his own and others' experience.

FEEDING

The most generally-kept pigeons and doves, the seed-eaters, are all very easily cared for. The small doves eat mostly milled and canary seeds; the larger ones, a mixture of wheat, kibbled corn (maize), and sorghum, to which may be added peas and rice. A little hemp is often useful in winter and just before the breeding season. Also all will enjoy soaked dog-biscuit, boiled rice, prepared pellets of various sorts, bread and milk, as well as broken peanuts and bread crumbs. But most species will thrive on the plainest diet of seeds only; grass growing in the aviary, also lettuce, chicory, and other greens are greatly appreciated. Salt should be supplied, mixed with sand or as rocksalt, as it helps to keep the birds in good

Sprouted seeds are good for any seed-eating bird, especially during the breeding season. Large sunflower seeds are generally not given to pigeons and doves, although smaller varieties of these seeds are available. Photo by Dr. H.R. Axelrod.

A domestic pigeon perched on a dish with food mixture containing gravel or grit. Crushed cuttlefish bone and egg-shells can also be included for their lime content. Photo by L. van der Meid.

health. Lime also must be available, in the form of prepared blocks, or otherwise. Doves are fond of cuttlefish bones and of crushed egg-shells.

While the great majority of seed-eating pigeons and doves can live and breed on a simple diet of grain and greens, a number of species, particularly those living on the ground, need some animal food and some fruit to replace the insects, grubs, and berries on which they largely fed in the wilds. While they can live without such soft food, they can hardly be expected to rear their squabs without it. Therefore, they should be given, at all times, soaked dog-biscuit, minced raw meat, or high-protein pellets, soaked raisins, and fresh fruit, such as apple and banana, in small quantities. They also like mealworms and maggots, which can be replaced by diced cheese—an excellent food. The more insectivorous and berry-eating species requiring soft food for successful breeding are the American Quail Doves *(Geotrygon* and allies*)* and the Pacific Ground Pigeons—Bleeding Hearts and allies.

Mourning Dove *(Zenaida macroura)*. This exclusively American dove is distributed over a wide area of North America, Central America, Cuba, Isle of Pines and Hispaniola. A San Diego Zoo photo.

Opposite, upper photo:
Talpacoti or Ruddy Ground Dove *(Columbina talpacoti)*. Photo courtesy of Vogelpark Walsrode.

Opposite, lower photo:
Galapagos Dove *(Nesopelia galapagoensis)*. This dove is limited to the Galapagos Islands. Some bird authorities prefer to place this species under the genus *Zenaida*. A San Diego Zoo photo.

A pair of doves near a nest built by themselves in a small aviary from materials available to them. Photo by L. van der Meid.

The Fruit Pigeons also eat dog-biscuit and pellets, which can be considered the staple food of many species, and all sorts of fruit cut up to swallowable size. Sticky fruit, notably bananas, should be rolled in bread crumbs or in corn meal, so that the birds' bills and faces do not become soiled. Soaked raisins, cut-up dates, and dried figs are excellent food, as are boiled rice and corn. Many Fruit Pigeons will also eat much grain. Though they consume a vast quantity of food, they are actually much easier to cater for than is often supposed.

BREEDING

A great many pigeons and doves want to breed as soon as the weather permits. In mild climates, many will nest throughout the year, both at liberty and in captivity; in the colder countries, they stop in the autumn and start again in the early spring, but a few will breed even in winter.

An aviary with an assortment of possible sites for building a nest: small and large nest boxes, wicker basket, wire strainer. Eggs often fall out of nests prepared by doves themselves. Photo by L. van der Meid.

Aviaries should be thoroughly cleaned no later than the middle of March: fresh perches should be made and boughs fixed, floors and shelters should be sanded, after washing them with hot water, disinfecting and polishing them thoroughly. If the aviary is well planted with shrubs and thick foliaged trees, doves will build in them without much trouble. But often they establish such flimsy platforms that the eggs or chicks may fall through. You must keep a close watch on their activities and strengthen their nests before it is too late. Often the birds will immediately accept a small basket fixed in the position of the dangerously weak nest. But many doves prefer to use baskets or boxes. Different sorts can be offered to them: baskets made of willow or reeds as sold for various uses; nests as made for canaries, only larger; and boxes made of wood, all to suit the size of the birds. These boxes can be open and low, or, if hung outdoors, covered with solid sides, back, and roof. It is advantageous to surround them with twigs, bundles of straw or

Peruvian Ground Dove *(Columbina cruziana).* On account of the color of the bill this dove is also called Yellow-billed or Gold-billed Ground Dove. A San Diego Zoo photo.

Opposite:
The brown coloration of the
Ruddy or Talpacoti Ground Dove
gives cause for some to call it
also the Cinnamon Dove. Photo
by H.V. Lacey.

sticks, and boughs to give them a more natural aspect. They should be lined with hay and grass, to which the doves will add small twigs and other material, such as bits of heather, short straws, and pine needles, which should be made available to them. These artificial nests are hung on the walls and partitions, or are fixed to the branches of the trees. The female builds the nest out of the material the male brings to her. If the nest is open and outside, it may be protected against rain by placing a pane of glass on the roof above it. Plenty of old mortar, crushed egg-shell, and oyster-shell will prevent egg-binding.

Incubation periods vary with species, but generally last eighteen days. After hatching, the young, or squabs, require no extra food or attention: the parents take care of them completely, provided that the supply of suitable food is sufficient. Young doves leave the nest before they can fly well. Then they squat on the ground, and you must make certain that they do not remain on damp soil, or are overexposed to rain. It is best to make them stay in the shelter on some dry litter. After a few days they can perch and fly about.

It sometimes happens that the parents, urged to breed again much too soon, abandon their young prematurely, and so let them die of starvation. To prevent such an accident, the new nest and eggs can be removed, or the cock and the hen separated, leaving one parent with the nestlings, or the squabs can be fed artificially. This is achieved by taking the bird's beak between the lips, when it will instinctively expect food, and pushing into the open jaw a mixture of seeds and bread crumbs. It is a fairly tedious and difficult performance, at which some breeders become exceedingly skillful. They can also be fed by the hand.

Some doves refuse to sit on their eggs or to rear their young when the accommodation does not suit them, when they want to nest again after incubating for a few days, or when they have been disturbed by cats, hawks, or other intruders. These abandoned eggs and squabs may be placed under other doves, which, being good sitters, will hatch and raise them. The domestic Ring Dove makes a good foster mother as does also the white variety; but if they are expected to rear the young of the more insectivorous Ground Doves, for instance, they should be trained, in advance, to eat high-protein foods. As the young Ground Doves leave the nest early, the Ring Doves which are expected to look after them should be kept in a low, long cage, with a nesting box placed on the ground; otherwise, they will cease to feed the young which have prematurely left the nest. This applies particularly to Plumed Doves, which are seldom hatched and fed by their own parents. Crested, Mourning, Senegal, and Spotted Doves have successfully reared other species of their own size or near their own size, while Diamond Doves are good foster parents for other small species. An experienced breeder has recommended the use of hybrids between Ring Doves and domestic pigeons, which are larger and which feed the young longer—a decided advantage. Furthermore, they are practically unsexed and sterile.

The late Marquis de Brisay, a great expert with doves, gives the following advice on installing these foster parents:

"The foster doves should be kept in pigeon holes arranged like a bookcase with two tiers, each compartment being about three feet

This pigeon has utilized an ordinary food strainer as its nest. The risk of the eggs falling out is very small, unless the nest is overturned. Photo by L. van der Meid.

Barred Dove *(Geopelia striata)*. Barred Doves are widely spread over the Indo-Malayan and Australasian regions. Several subspecies are known.

Opposite:
Bar-shouldered Dove *(Geopelia humeralis)*. The nest of this dove found in northern and eastern Australia and southern New Guinea is built above the ground in low trees and shrubs. Photo by K. Hindwood.

A mother pigeon watching her eggs hatch. Broken twigs, straw, feathers, etc., are used to line the nest. Photo by L. van der Meid.

square. I have a sort of cupboard six feet high, six feet wide, and three feet deep, divided by cross partitions into four separate compartments. All the sides of those boxes are made of board; the front is wired and the interior communicates with the outside by a sliding door on one side of each compartment. This cage is protected from wind, rain, and cold in a warm, well-lighted room with very good aeration. One pair of foster doves is placed in each compartment with a basket filled with hay. As soon as eggs are laid, they are removed and replaced by those intended to be hatched. They may be given even half-grown nestlings which their own parents have forsaken. The foster parents must be used to feeding on a mixture of millet, maize, and hemp, on bread and milk, chopped, hard-boiled eggs, insects, maggots, and mealworms. It is in this way that the best results are obtained."

In the past many breeders have raised large numbers of rare doves by the use of well-selected and well-fed foster parents. This method, which is habitually used today in California for the rearing of Plumed Doves, should be more generally adopted. But it can be successful only if the foster Ring Doves are properly housed and fed.

In places where birds of prey and other predators are under control, it is often possible to keep doves at liberty. A number of species, which do not migrate, will stay in a garden as long as food and protection are available. Some species are thus easily established. Such is the case with the Chinese Spotted Turtle Dove throughout Los Angeles, Calif., where it is now very common, and with the domestic Ring Dove in the heart of the same city. The latter is defenseless and can succeed only where no competiton of any kind exists. At Cleres, and in other parks in France and in England, the following species have lived and bred free for many years: Australian Crested, Senegal, Spotted, Indian Ring, Pea, and Martinique Doves.

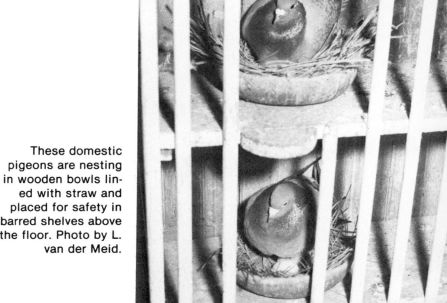

These domestic pigeons are nesting in wooden bowls lined with straw and placed for safety in barred shelves above the floor. Photo by L. van der Meid.

Zebra Dove *(Geopelia s. striata)* is the race of Barred Dove found in the Indo-Malayan region. Photo courtesy of Vogelpark Walsrode.

Opposite:
This dove at the San Diego Zoo has decided to utilize the ready-made nest of a weaver, instead of building one of its own. Photo by Dr. Herbert R. Axelrod.

The author in the process of hanging a wicker basket for fruit-eating doves. Note the fruit secured on the wall of this aviary. Photo by L. van der Meid.

The worst danger to pigeons and doves at liberty comes from hawks and owls during the winter, particularly Cooper Hawks and great horned owls in America, sparrow hawks and brown owls in Europe. These predators must be strictly controlled. When possible, it is a good plan to catch the doves in October or November, and to liberate them again in April. All the species tried multiplied fast and soon became numerous. The males of the Australian Crested, however, are very quarrelsome during the breeding season, which extends to most months of the year, and young pairs are chased away by the father as soon as they become adults. Other species were tried successfully at Woburn Abbey by the late Duke of Bedford *(Avic. Magazine,* 1914).

DISEASES

Not only are the diseases of aviary birds still little understood, but in many cases the remedies are unknown. Fortunately, doves are healthy creatures and provided they are well cared for, subject to little serious illness.

Diarrhea, which is usually caused by long-continued damp, can generally be cured by keeping the affected bird dry and warm, and removing all laxative food. A cold should be dealt with in the same way: a few drops of glycerine mixed with the drinking water makes a good medicine, and a little syrup of iron phosphate is an excellent tonic. Constipation, which is not common, can be treated by giving tepid olive oil. Miss Rosie Alderson, of England, advises also giving drops of oil introduced into the vent in cases of egg-binding, which, however, do not often occur among doves.

Fits, usually caused by blows or sudden fright, are rare. The sufferer should be kept cool, sprinkled with cold water, and made to drink a little brandy and water. Afterwards, the bird should have Vichy water for some days. I think sunstroke is often mistaken for apoplectic fits. It is advisable to shade aviaries exposed to full sun by laying leafy branches on the netting during the heat of the day. Pneumonia, which sometimes occurs after violent changes of temperature, is nearly always incurable.

The worst disease which attacks pigeons is diphtheria. It is to be dreaded all the more, because it is more contagious and can be communicated to every pigeon throughout the aviary. It shows itself in different ways, but is always accompanied by membranes in the throat, which are white at first, then become yellow; as the disease progresses, the bird has more and more difficulty swallowing. The only remedy against pigeon diphtheria is injection of a special serum. The amount to be injected varies with the size of the bird. I have never had to use this vaccine on my foreign pigeons, but numerous breeders of domestic and fancy pigeons have successfully used it.

Today there are new and very effective remedies, particularly antibiotics, which can be employed successfully in many infectious cases, such as canker of the throat, which is common among domestic pigeons kept in dirty surroundings and which sometimes affects wild species as well.

Left:
Diamond Dove
(Geopelia cuneata).
This is the smallest
of doves; it is also
called Little Dove or
Little Turtledove.
Photo courtesy of
Vogelpark Walsrode.
Below:
Zebra Doves in cap-
tivity will accept
other foods not found
in nature, like bread
and biscuits. A San
Diego Zoo photo.

For breeding in captivity Diamond Doves can be provided with a typical pigeon's nest, only smaller in size. Photo by H.V. Lacey.

Bronze-winged Pigeons and Doves

The birds of this group are handsome, easy to keep and to breed, and have long been popular in aviaries. They are stoutly built and possess beautiful, metallic spots or patches on the wings. They spend much of their time on the ground; indeed, some are among the most terrestrial birds of the family. All species lay two eggs, creamy-white or buff. They can be fed on various seeds, such as millet, sorghum, wheat, and corn; but some of the larger species like insects and other soft food. They are found in Africa, southern Asia, Malaysia, south to Australia and New Guinea.

The CAPE or MASKED DOVE *(Oena capensis)* is a graceful little species common in savannas, gardens, farms, and cattle yards throughout Africa, Madagascar, and Arabia. It runs quickly on the ground in search of seeds, flies fast, but often hovers like a butterfly, and it is tame and quiet in disposition. The Cape Dove has a long, pointed tail. The male is brownish gray above, more ashy on the crown, neck, and wing-coverts, the latter with steel-blue patches; quills cinnamon; two black bands on the rump; front part of the head and throat black; breast and belly white; bill red with a yellow tip. The female is duller and has no black on the face. This little dove is often kept and bred in captivity. The young are easy to rear, if they do not jump out of the nest at too early an age. Cape Doves are gentle and harmless to other birds, fairly hardy in cold countries.

The TAMBOURINE DOVE *(Turtur tympanistria)* is a charming bird of fairly small size with a rather short tail. It is native to the wooded districts of Africa, from Abyssinia and Sierra Leone south to the Cape of Good Hope. This dove feeds on fallen seeds, as well as on insects and small snails. It has a very peculiar coo, which sounds like a tom-tom. The male's upper-parts are dark

Front view of a
Cape Dove
(Oena capensis),
also called
Masked Dove
on account of
its marking.
Photo by Elvie.

brownish gray, the wings spotted with metallic green and purple; quills cinnamon; forehead, eyebrows, cheeks and the under-parts are pure white. The female has black wing spots and grayish under-parts. Tambourine Doves are not often imported and remain scarce in aviaries. They are, however, inclined to breed in captivity, and young birds have been reared on many occasions: Steinbeck, Strann, and Naether in California have raised numbers of them. They are quiet little birds, living in peace with other species, and they are attractive.

The BLUE-SPOTTED DOVE *(Turtur afer)* comes from West and East Africa. It is a near relative of the Tambourine, but frequents more open country. It has a monotonous coo- "Tor, tor-tor, tor-tor-tor-tor . . ." Both sexes are alike, earthy-brown above with two black bars on the lower back; the wings have metallic blue spots; crown gray, whitish on the forehead; neck and breast pale vinous, fading to whitish on the belly; bill gray, with an orange tip. The female is slightly smaller and paler, but difficult to tell from the male. This little dove is not very ornamental, but it is quiet and tame. It is often imported and breeds fairly readily.

A very similar species is found in Abyssinia *(T. abyssinica)* but its bill is wholly black.

Diamond Doves are kept and bred in aviaries all over the world. As with most other domesticated animals, new varieties through mutations and selection can be expected. Top photo courtesy of San Diego Zoo, lower photo by P. Kwast.

Eastern Turtle Dove *(Streptopelia orientalis meena).* The illustration
represents the race or form found in the western Himalayas.

The EMERALD-SPOTTED DOVE *(Turtur chalcospilos)* is found from the Congo, Angola and Abyssinia to the Cape, in dry parts at low altitudes. The nest is seldom placed at any great height from the ground. The coo is similar to that of the Blue-spotted Dove, but softer— "Hoo, hoo-hoo-hoooo . . ." This dove resembles the Blue-spotted, but it is a little smaller and brighter, and the wing spots are metallic green; the bill is black. A more attractive bird, it is equally suitable for aviaries, where it has bred on several occasions. It is fairly rare in captivity.

The MAIDEN DOVE *(T. brehmeri)* is larger and lives in the forests of West Africa, from Sierra Leone to the Congo. It is a secretive bird, seldom seen and rarely imported. It was bred in the London Zoo a few years ago. I have kept several pairs of these lovely doves at Cleres in France, and they have nested. They are susceptible to cold, and I believe they would do better in southern California. However, none have bred there, although several pairs arrived some years ago. Both sexes are alike: the head is skyblue, the body cinnamon, with large, metallic spots on the wings. It is a beautiful species.

The GREEN-WINGED DOVE *(Chalcophaps indica)* is one of the most brightly-colored species of seed-eating pigeons. It lives in dense bush and forest. Although common in many parts of its range, it is shy and not easily seen. This species feeds on the ground on fallen seeds and berries. It flies very fast through the branches, eluding pursuit by dropping suddenly to the ground and remaining still. Green-winged Doves are found throughout India, Ceylon, east to Indochina, and the Philippines, and south to Australia and New Guinea. Their plumage is beautiful: head, neck, and under-parts rich vinous, with a purple tint on the nape and hind-neck; mantle bright coppery green; lower back blackish, with two gray bands; tail gray with a broad, black tip. The male has a bluish gray crown, white eyebrows, forehead and patches on bend of wing, and a red bill. There are some local races, especially one in Australia and New Guinea *(chrysochlora)*, in which the male has neither the white nor gray on the head, but a larger white patch on the bend of the wing. All females lack the white eyebrows and wing-patches.

Green-winged Doves have long been favorites with bird fanciers. They are hardy, easy to maintain and to breed, as well as

Green-winged Dove *(Chalcophaps indica)*. This species is also called Emerald Dove and was first described by Linnaeus. Photo by Elvie.

quiet and peaceful with other species. Common in captivity, there is not a more charming dove that you can keep. They nest readily, if rather irregularly, rearing several broods in a short time, then stopping for several months.

STEPHANI'S GREEN-WINGED DOVE *(Chalcophaps stephani)*, from Celebes, New Guinea, and neighboring islands, differs from other green-winged doves in that the middle of the back and scapulars are cinnamon-rufous, with only the wings green, the tail rufous-brown, and a large, white patch on the forehead, which in the female is gray. It has the same habits as the preceding species, and it is not rare in its native islands. It has been imported infrequently. I have kept a few at Cleres, France, but to my knowledge they have never nested.

The WHITE-FRONTED PIGEON *(Henicophaps albifrons)*, from New Guinea and nearby islands, is of large size, with a very long, strong beak and a short tail. It is very wild and wary, and lives on the forest floor, perching now and then on tall trees. Its general color is a slate-gray, with green reflections on the mantle and a large green patch on the wing, bordered with chestnut; its forehead is white.

This remarkable, but rather coarse, species has been imported occasionally. I have kept it, but it remains so wild and is so rough

Left and below:
Views of the Indian
Ring Dove *(Strep-
topelia decaocto),*
domestic pied variety.
Photos by Dr. Herbert
R. Axelrod.

The colored feathers in the pied variety of Indian Ring Dove vary in size and position, but the collar is unchanged. Photo by Dr. Herbert R. Axelrod.

in disposition that it is hardly worth keeping. To my knowledge, it has not been bred in captivity. It is quite easy to maintain on grain.

The BRONZE-WINGED PIGEON *(Phaps chalcoptera)* is a fine bird, widely distributed in Australia. It is common in open bush country, where it feeds on the ground on the seeds of acacia and other trees. When disturbed, it flies rapidly to a nearby tree. The nest is built near the ground, on horizontal, often hollow branches of trees. The male's forehead is ochraceous-yellow, the crown grayish-brown, purplish on the sides, a whitish line below the eye extending across the ear coverts. Its upper-parts are brown, with light borders to the feathers; the wing-coverts have large, very bright metallic patches of copper-red or green, according to the light, producing a magnificent effect. The inner secondaries have shining violet patches changing to blue-green; the cheeks and sides of neck are bluish-gray; forehead buff; throat white; breast vinous, passing to gray on the belly; bill black. The female lacks the buff forehead and the vinous breast. The male's coo is deep, and he spreads his wings and tail in display. It is a satisfactory aviary bird, breeding freely, usually tame.

The BRUSH BRONZE-WINGED PIGEON *(Phaps elegans)* is a little smaller and shorter. It also inhabits Australia, but it lives in thicker, damper bush than the common Bronze-wing. It is a beautiful olive-gray bird, with its hind-neck and upper-back chestnut; two broad, copper-green and purple bands on the wings; forehead ochre-yellow; crown gray; a chestnut band from eye to nape; under-parts gray. The female is duller, lacking the yellow forehead, and she has little chestnut on the neck. Brush Bronze-wings are excellent aviary birds and breed well. One pair reared six broods of two young in one year in my Los Angeles, Calif., aviaries. Fertile hybrids between Brush and Common Bronze-wings have been raised.

The CRESTED PIGEON *(Ocyphaps lophotes)* is widespread and common in Australia; the sexes are alike. They are found in bush, forest, and garden. The plumage is gray, barred with black above; the greater wing-coverts are metallic green with white borders, the secondaries metallic violet and blue, also edged with white; the tail is long, as is the pointed head crest. This very handsome species is hardy and strong, and a free border. But it is quar-

The Crested Pigeon *(Ocyphaps lophotes)* is a common species in Australia, found almost throughout that continent. Photo by Elvie.

relsome and dangerous to weaker doves. The male spreads his wings and tail when displaying. This dove flies swiftly and with a strong, whirring note. In England it has been successfully established at liberty for several years, also in France. It is common in captivity.

The PLUMED DOVE *(Lophophaps plumifera)* inhabits the dry interior of Australia. There are two main forms—one with a white, the other with a chestnut, belly. It is abundant in suitable localities, among rocks and hot, sandy gullies, eating the seeds of spinifex and other plants, and nesting on the ground. It has typically terrestrial habits. It is a small, short dove with a strong, straight bill and a very long, pointed, upstanding crest—altogether a quaint and beautiful bird. Its general color is cinnamon-red, the upper parts barred with dark brown; the forehead and ear coverts are gray, the crown and crest cinnamon, the cheeks and throat white; the chin, a line over the eyes and a gorget black; a grayish-white band across the chest and metallic blue patches on the wings. The skin around the eyes is bare and red. Sexes are alike in color, but the female is a little smaller.

The collar of this white variety of Indian Ring Dove is very slightly
indicated as a pale band, whereas in another specimen of a pied variety *(facing page)* the collar is much darker than any other part of
the plumage. Photos by Dr. Herbert R. Axelrod.

The white-bellied variety is often kept in captivity. Though Plumed Doves are tame and very interesting in their ways, they are so bad-tempered that it is impossible to keep them with weaker doves. They lay abundantly, but seldom brood. For this reason, it is usually necessary to give their eggs to foster parents, such as domestic Ring Doves. Since the young Plumed Doves leave the nest very early, precautions must be taken to induce the foster parents to continue feeding them. Sometimes it is necessary to complete their rearing by hand. This lovely little bird is raised in fair numbers in California at present.

The PARTRIDGE BRONZE-WINGED PIGEON *(Geophaps scripta)* of Eastern Australia, also called Squatter Pigeon, is a purely terrestrial species of moderate size with the habits of a partridge or a quail. Contrary to the Plumed Dove, it is peaceful, quiet, and not aggressive. It moves about in small flocks; when disturbed, the individuals scatter, endeavoring to hide by squatting near a rock; they are then difficult to detect and to flush. Their nest is made on the ground, sometimes in a tuft of grass. The sexes are alike; their general color is pale brown, the tips of the feathers paler on the wings, which have a patch of metallic purple-geen; a narrow strip above and in front of the eyes, cheeks, throat, and a band on each side of the breast, white; two black bands across the sides of the head run into another one which borders the white cheeks; the underparts are gray. It is a desirable species in captivity owing to its gentleness and interesting habits, but it remains rare and unavailable. It is, however, inclined to breed in the proper environment, such as rocks and rough grass; it incubates well and rears its young readily. When hatched, the chicks have no more down than other squabs, but they leave the nest and walk about at an early age. There is a well-developed egg-tooth, or hard tip, to both mandibles of the bill, which persists for a long time. The young begin to molt before the first plumage is complete so that the bird attains its adult livery when it is completely grown.

SMITH'S PARTRIDGE PIGEON *(Geophaps smithi)* is found in small flocks in the bush country of North and Northwest Australia. When flushed, these birds fly to the nearest tree, choosing a large, horizontal branch to perch on, rest a few seconds, then dash out of sight. But often they allow themselves to be nearly stepped on before rising. They lay in a shallow depression of the ground. Their main diet consists mostly of acacia seeds. They resemble *scripta,* but are smaller and of a more uniform brown, with a large, rosy-red bare space around the eyes surrounded by a black line. There is a light gray patch on the middle of the breast, the feathers being tipped with black, giving a barred appearance; the sides of the breast are white. This quaint ground pigeon is seldom imported, which is a pity, as it is tame, quiet, peaceful and a ready breeder.

The HARLEQUIN PIGEON *(Histriophaps histrionica)* is known also as the Flock Pigeon in Australia owing to its sudden appearance in large flocks when grass seeds are plentiful. It inhabits the open, dry plains of the interior, nesting on the bare ground under a low bush. These pigeons fly over the surface, take a hasty drink, and depart. They have short legs and stand close to the ground like sandgrouse, which they resemble more than any other pigeon, having the same long wings and general sandy color. The male is light cinnamon-brown above, with edge of wing and quills gray, the latter tipped with white; a patch of purple and green on the wing; tail gray, black, and white; crown, sides of face, ear-coverts, and throat black; forehead, a line around the ear coverts, a patch below the throat pure white; under-parts gray, washed with cinnamon on flanks and vent. The female lacks the black-and-white markings on the head. This very beautiful ground pigeon has seldom been imported, although it was bred at the London Zoo in 1886, and in France in 1881. A pair recently brought to California never nested. It is a nomadic species, which disappears for years before showing up in large numbers. It was thought extinct several times.

The ROCK DOVES *(Petrophassa)* inhabit the sandstone ranges of North and Northwestern Australia. They live on the ground, are hard to flush and easily overlooked as they crouch near rocks, with which their color harmonizes well. They nest on the ground. They are dull-colored, dark rufous-brown, barred lighter; lores black; head and neck grayer; the feathers of the chin and throat tipped with white; a metallic violet patch on the wing. One form *(albipennis)* has the base of its quills white, while another one *(rufipennis)* has chestnut. These doves have almost never been imported, except for a single specimen in the London Zoo in 1910. They are not attractive.

European Turtle Dove *(Streptopelia turtur)*. These birds are known to hybridize with the Ring or Barbary Doves. Photo courtesy of Vogelpark Walsrode.

These Indian Ring Doves have mostly white feathers, except for those at the tips of the wings and tail. A San Diego Zoo photo.

The silver mutation is one of the earliest to have appeared in the Indian Ring Dove. Studies have shown that wild populations of this species have spread widely and have become very dependent on man for their food supply. Photo by H.V. Lacey.

American Doves

A large group of doves live exclusively in the Americas; they also can be called Zenaida Doves. The typical species is the well-known Mourning Dove, common throughout the United States. The extinct Passenger Pigeon *(Ectopistes migratorius)* also belonged to this group, of which it was by far the largest species.

A few of these doves have long, pointed tails, while others, often very similar otherwise, have fairly short and rounded tails. American doves somewhat resemble the Bronze-wings in having metallic black or purple spots on the wings; they resemble also the Old World Turtle Doves *(Streptopelia)* and the Malay and Australian Ground Doves *(Geopelia)*. All are pretty in a quiet way; a few *(Claravis)* are decidedly beautiful. They live and breed very well in captivity. Being almost wholly granivorous, they feed on millet, wheat, cracked corn, and other grains. Most of them are hardy, enduring even cold weather.

The MOURNING DOVE *(Zenaida macroura)*, the common North American dove, is abundant and popular in the United States, Canada, the temperate sections of Mexico, and the Greater Antilles. There are several local races, but they are very much alike. In winter, the northern birds migrate south as far as Panama. The *mourning* in Mourning Dove relates to the sad coo, "Ho-woe-woe-woe!" These birds are brown above, with black spots on the wings and scapulars. The head is reddish, with a black spot behind the eyes and another one below on the ear-coverts; the sides of the neck are glossed with a metallic purplish-lilac; under-parts pale reddish-brown; the breast purplish; tail long and pointed, the feathers black at the base, the outer ones tipped with white, the others with pale tips, becoming bluer towards the middle feathers, which are brown. The female is slightly duller. Mourning Doves are very easy to keep, perfectly hardy and free breeders in aviaries.

GRAYSON'S DOVE *(Zenaida graysoni)* is found on the small island of Socorro, off the Pacific Coast of Mexico. It is larger and redder than the Mourning Dove. Its under-parts are deep rufous-cinnamon; and it is decidedly brighter and prettier. It is tame by nature, but also very quarrelsome. Breeding pairs are best isolated, or placed with stronger birds only, as they will kill weaker species. A pair at Cleres killed Pennant's parrakeets, large and powerful Australian birds. Grayson's Doves are commonly kept and bred in captivity.

PEA DOVES *(Zenaida auriculata)* are abundant throughout South America. There are many local races which differ only slightly from one another. Often they congregate in large flocks and migrate to the south of their range, but mostly they move about in quest of food according to seasons. They frequently nest near houses as a protection against hawks. They resemble Mourning Doves in color, but their crown is gray; the sides of neck and nape have golden reflections; the tail is rounded and not very long, grayish-brown, with a black band across the middle, the three outer pairs of feathers having white tips. The female is somewhat duller. Pea Doves have been imported frequently and breed easily in aviaries.

The MARTINIQUE DOVE *(Zenaida z. aurita)* is common in the Lesser Antilles. It is a larger, brighter bird: upper-parts brown, the wings with black spots edged with white; a white band at the tip of the secondaries; head vinous-rufous, with two steel-blue spots; metallic black patches on the back of the neck; breast cinnamon, fading to white under the tail; outer tail-feathers black at base with white tips; the tail is rounded. This dove, often imported, thrives in captivity.

A slightly different subspecies *(Z. z. zenaida)* inhabits the Greater Antilles and is darker, with no white edges to the black wing spots.

The WHITE-WINGED DOVE *(Zenaida asiatica)* is found in a few slightly different forms from the southwestern United States through the Greater Antilles and Mexico to Central America and the Pacific Coast of South America to Chile. In this last area, it is larger and shows less gray in the tail *(Z. a. meloda)*. This fair-sized dove with rounded tail has the upper-parts, throat and breast

When surrounded by much foliage a Crested Pigeon may be difficult to see. Except for the bright orange-red eye, bright colors are nowhere else to be seen in this grayish brown bird. A San Diego Zoo photo.

Oppƿsite:
An albino form of the Barbary Dove.
Photo by Harry V. Lacey.

grayish-brown; a broad, white band on the wing; secondaries blackish, margined with white; head purplish-gray, shot with green on the sides of the neck; a black stripe below the ears; central tail-feathers brown, the others dark gray, tipped with whitish. The female is less purplish on the head. This dove does well in captivity.

GALAPAGOS DOVES *(Nesopelia galapagoensis)* live on the dry rocks of those islands. They are extraordinarily tame. Rather small, the male is a good deal larger than the female; their tails are short. General coloring is a brownish-olive, the scapulars and upper wing-coverts brown, with a white center and a black spot on each side. Crown of head, breast, and abdomen vinous; ear-coverts whitish, with a black stripe above and below; tail brown, with a black bar across the middle. The blue skin—eye cere—is very showy.

These pretty little doves are very interesting in their ways: they spend much time on the ground; they are inquisitive and quarrelsome, and must be watched when kept with other birds. They nest among rocks. Suitable nesting sites—recessed in rocks and boxes—should be provided. In California they have bred freely, also in Europe. However, after a few generations, they become sterile.

The BLACK-WINGED DOVE *(Metriopelia melanoptera)* inhabits the Andes at high altitudes in open country and on bare slopes. It is small, grayish-brown, with the sides of neck and breast pale buff, wing and tail blackish. Among.the several other species of the same genus in the Andes are *M. ceciliae,* which I had at Cleres, *M. morenoi,* and *M. aymara.* All are quaint little ground dwellers, seldom, if ever, found in aviaries.

The SCALY DOVE *(Scardafella squamata)* from Brazil is a small ground species, grayish-brown above, white below; all its feathers are edged with black; the wing has a white patch. The tail is long; sexes are alike. It lives and breeds well in captivity. A somewhat paler race *(S. s. ridgwayi)* lives in Colombia and Venezuela.

INCA DOVES *(Scardafella inca)* inhabit the southwestern United States, Mexico, and Central America. They closely resemble the Scaly Doves, but are browner, less heavily barred, and have no white wing-patch. Familiar birds, they are often seen in gardens and near buildings. They thrive in captivity, but both species of *Scardafella* are inclined to become abnormally blackish if too closely confined.

PICUI DOVES *(Columbina picui)* from Brazil, Argentina, Uruguay, Bolivia, and Chile are pretty little birds; their crown and nape are gray; upper-parts ashy brown; wing-coverts and secondaries edged with white, and a band of steel-blue across the lesser coverts; sides of head, neck, and under-parts pale vinaceous; chin and center of belly white. The female is browner, without any gray on head or any vinaceous below. Eyes lilac. Picuis are tame and flourish in aviaries, where they breed easily and prove harmless to other birds.

PASSERINE GROUND DOVES *(Columbina passerina)* are well known from the southern United States to Ecuador and Central Brazil, including the West Indies and other islands. There are numerous local races which all resemble one another, the differences being degrees of size and of color. One sees them on the roads, in yards, gardens, and on open ground, or else perching on telephone wires and on houses. They nest anywhere from the ground up to fifteen feet or more in trees. These small, rather short-tailed doves have the top of the head and hind-neck bluish-gray, the feathers margined with dusky gray; their upper-parts are plain grayish-brown, with metallic purplish-black wing-spots; primaries chestnut, bordered by black; forehead, sides of head, neck and under-parts vinous-gray, the feathers of the breast with dark borders, producing a scaly effect. The female is duller, lacking the vinous tinge underneath. These little doves are excellent aviary birds and breed freely.

The PIGMY GROUND DOVE *(Columbina minuta)* is the smallest of the group, no bigger than the Australian Diamond Doves, but it has a short tail. The male is brownish-gray, with a vinous tinge on the wing-coverts and the under-parts, and steel-blue dots on the wings. The female is a good deal browner, with a little gray tinge. This dove inhabits Mexico, Central and South America south to central Brazil, Paraguay, and coastal Peru. It is one of the nicest small doves to keep and to breed. Several little marked races include:

BUCKLEY'S GROUND DOVE *(Columbina buckleyi)* is much like the Pigmy, but more vinaceous, less gray. It has carmine eyes

Above and below: African Ring Dove *(Streptopelia roseogrisea).*
Photos by Dr. Herbert R. Axelrod at the San Diego Zoo.

Dwarf Turtle Dove *(Streptopelia tranquebarica)*. The form illustrated here *(S. t. humilis)* is called Red Turtle Dove because the male is predominantly red, although the female is not.

Peruvian Ground Dove *(Columbina cruziana)*. Although this species is of very limited distribution in the wild, it has been successfully bred in captivity in America and Europe. Photo by Elvie.

and is found in the hot country of western Ecuador and northern Peru. It has seldom been imported.

TALPACOTI or RUDDY GROUND DOVE *(Columbina talpacoti)*, a little larger, is vinaceous-red, paler below, with top of head and nape gray. Its wings are marked with steel-blue spots. This very attractive dove is common from Mexico to Argentina and Peru. Among the several local races are the Mexican *(rufipennis)*. Its quills are cinnamon, tipped with brown; the female is dull brown, while the South American birds' quills are mainly black, the female being only slightly duller than the male. Both Mexican and South American Talpacotis have frequently been imported and reared in Europe and in the United States.

The PERUVIAN GROUND DOVE *(Columbina cruziana)*, about the size of the Talpacoti, is one of the most attractive and easiest small dove to keep and to breed. Before Dr. E. W. Gifford of Oakland, Calif., imported and bred this dove, it had been unknown in captivity. It is now common in both American and European aviaries, but as far as is known, only four specimens had previously been sent to the London Zoo, in 1915. It inhabits the dry coast of the Pacific from northern Ecuador to northern Chile, where it is very common. The male's call is a peculiar grunt, very unlike that of any dove. Peruvian Doves are active, but can bother smaller species. The male has a gray head, brownish-gray upper-parts, steel-blue spots on the wings, as well as a beautiful chestnut-purple band across the lesser coverts; the under-parts are pinkish-vinaceous; the bill is yellow, with a black tip. The female is duller, practically all brown with the same wing markings.

All species of *Columbina,* although active and even quarrelsome, can live and breed in colonies in a large, planted aviary.

The BLUE GROUND DOVE *(Claravis pretiosa)* is still larger. The male is bluish-gray, the forehead, throat, and under-parts whitish; primaries and tip of tail are black, the wings have large, blue-black patches. The female is cinnamon-brown, with dark brown wing-patches. Both sexes are very handsome in their different livery. Their habitat ranges from southern Mexico to Peru, Bolivia, and Argentina, but they are not very common anywhere. They do well in captivity, being quiet and harmless, and they breed regularly.

GEOFFREY'S GROUND DOVE *(Claravis godefrida),* from southern Brazil and Paraguay, is similar in both sexes, but much larger, about the size of a Mourning Dove, its wings crossed by four purplish bands. It lives well in captivity. Formerly, it came frequently to Europe, where it bred easily. None have been there or in the United States for a long time. It is a very desirable species.

A third species *(Claravis mondetoura),* intermediate in size and even more handsomely colored, inhabits the mountains of southern Mexico, Central America, Colombia, Venezuela, Ecuador, and Peru. This most interesting dove has, apparently, not been kept in captivity.

Two central Brazilian species are also unknown in captivity—the very rare BLUE-EYED DOVE *(Oxypelia cyanopis)* and the more common LONG-TAILED DOVE *(Uropelia campestris).* Both are quaint, handsome, and well worth trying to import and breed.

Malay Spotted Turtle Dove *(Streptopelia c. tigrina)*, the race found in Burma and Malayan regions.

Opposite:
Chinese Spotted Turtle Dove
(Streptopelia chinensis chinensis). A San Diego Zoo photo.

Turtle Doves

LONG-TAILED GROUND DOVES

There are in Malaysia and in Australia three species of doves of the genus *Geopelia*, which, like the American species just reviewed, spend much time on the ground. One is the size of a Mourning Dove, while the other two are very small. All have long tails and black bars or white spots in their plumage, but no metallic patches on the wings. They thrive in captivity, where they are very popular, the attractive and diminutive Diamond Dove being almost domesticated. The sexes are similar, the females being only slightly smaller and less brightly colored.

The BAR-SHOULDERED DOVE *(Geopelia humeralis)* inhabits eastern and nothern Australia, with a slightly different subspecies in southern New Guinea. This, the large species of the genus, abounds in thickets, swampy ground, and on the banks of streams. A handsome dove, with the front portion of its head, neck, and upper-breast bluish-gray; crown and nape bright cinnamon, barred with black. The remaining upper-parts are brown, barred with black; the lower breast is lilac, fading to white on the vent; the tail is pointed, its outer feathers being rufous-chestnut tipped with white. Bar-shouldered Doves are hardy and breed readily in aviaries. Since they are inclined to fight, each pair should be isolated, or else kept only with stronger birds. In very large pens, however, several pairs may be kept together successfully.

Several subspecies of BARRED DOVES *(Geopelia striata)* are distributed from the Malay Peninsula to the Philippines and to Australia. All are small, attractive, and do very well in captivity.

The ZEBRA DOVE *(G. s. striata)* is found in Tenasserim, the Malay Peninsula, the Philippines, Borneo, Sumatra, Java, east to Lombock. It has been introduced into St. Helena, Hawaii, and

Zebra Doves *(Geopelia striata striata)*. Photo by Elvie.

other islands. It is very numerous in open country and in gardens. Naturally tame, these birds usually feed in pairs on grass seeds and nest in bushes and hedges. Their forehead, cheeks, and throat are ashy-gray; the occiput reddish; neck and breast finely barred with black and white; the upper-parts are brown with thin, black bars, the center of the breast is vinous, passing to white below the tail, the outer feathers of which are black with broad, white tips. Young birds have the lower-parts barred and lack the vinaceous tinge on the breast. The skin around the eyes is pale blue. Zebra Doves nest easily in aviaries, but they are quarrelsome with other small doves.

MAUGE'S DOVE *(G. s. maugei)* is found in the Lesser Sunda Islands, east of Lombock, including Sumba and Timor. It is much like the Zebra Dove, but has no vinous on the breast, which, as well as the neck, is barred. The bare skin about the eyes is chrome-yellow. It has been bred at Cleres, and in the London Zoo as early as 1867. Though this pretty subspecies is easy to cater for, it is seldom obtainable.

Left:
Senegal Palm Turtle Dove *(Streptopelia senegalensis senegalensis).* Photo courtesy of Vogelpark, Walsrode.

Below:
Indian race of Palm Turtle Dove *(Streptopelia s. cambayensis).*

Bar-tailed Cuckoo Dove *(Macropygia unchall)*. Photo by A.J. Mobbs.

PEACEFUL DOVES *(G. s. placida)* live in northern Australia and southern New Guinea, while a somewhat larger and darker form *(tranquila)* inhabits the remainder of Australia. Both are kept in aviaries and often confused, owing to their very slight differences. They are a little longer in shape than the Zebra Doves and their barring on the under-parts is confined to the crop region. Their eyes are ringed in blue. Peaceful Doves are common in meadows and along streams in flocks of from twenty to fifty. In captivity they breed freely, and unlike Zebra Doves, they are quiet and do not harm other species. Today they are reared commercially in France, one pair usually kept with a pair of Diamond Doves and a number of budgerigars, zebras, or other finches in the same pen.

The DIAMOND DOVE *(Geopelia cuneata)*, the smallest and one of the prettiest of all doves, is also the most popular. It is abundant in Australia along rivers in the bush country. Its head, neck and breast are pearl-gray; nape, back scapulars pale brown; wing-coverts gray, spotted with white dots. The tail is dark gray, its outer feathers tipped with white; the under-parts are pale gray, and the eye cere is red. Diamond Doves are reared in large numbers, both in America and in Europe, and no more satisfactory little birds can be found in captivity. Moreover, they are ideal for keeping with finches. In a sufficiently large aviary several pairs will breed, although they may quarrel at times. Better results are obtained by keeping only one pair in a pen with zebra and other Australian or African finches. They get along nicely also with other quiet species of doves, painted quail, etc. This semi-domestic dove is beginning to produce mutations like the budgerigar, the canary, and the zebra finch: a silver variety, much paler than the original type, is already well established.

THE TURTLE DOVES

The members of the genus *Streptopelia* are distributed throughout Europe, Africa, and Asia, southeast to Java and east to Japan and the Philippines, but none are found in Australia, the Pacific islands, or the Americas. These doves are medium in size and proportions. All have either a dark collar or scale-like patches on the neck, but neither the metallic spots on the wing nor purple or green reflections on the neck. There are numerous different

In appearance Diamond Doves *(Geopelia cuneata)* are just as pretty and small as many of the popular finches. Furthermore, they are all compatible when kept in a large aviary. Photo by H.V. Lacey.

species, all which live and breed well in captivity. One species, the Ring or Barbary Dove, has long been domesticated and is too well known to need description. The pure white variety is also well known.

The EUROPEAN TURTLE DOVE *(Streptopelia turtur)*, which breeds in Europe and Asia as far north as Scotland and Russia, wintering in West Africa, is popular in Europe, where its deep-purring coo, "rroorr, rroorr" is very familiar. Its head is bluish-gray; a patch of black feathers tipped with pale gray on each side of the neck; the mantle is brown, the feathers edged with rufous; the rest of the upper-parts is tinged with bluish-gray; rump and tail dark blue-gray, the lateral tail-feathers tipped with white; chin, throat, and breast vinous; the belly and under tail-coverts are white. Turtle doves live well in captivity and can endure any cold

Himalayan race of Bar-tailed Cuckoo Dove *(Macropygia u. tusalia)*.

Opposite:
A Palm Turtle Dove *(Streptopelia senegalensis)* in captivity. Photo by H.V. Lacey.

climate in spite of their migratory habits. Though they breed easily, they remain wild and are inclined to bang their heads. They cross freely with Barbary or Ring doves, the hybrids being fertile.

Numerous races of Turtle Doves inhabit various islands, North Africa, western Asia *(arenicola)*, and Egypt *(isabellina)*. A larger, brighter, but otherwise similar, species *(Streptopelia orientalis)* breeds in central and eastern Siberia, south to the Himalayas, southern China, and east to Japan, wintering in eastern India, Indochina, Formosa, and Hainan. Another race *(meena)* breeds in western Siberia, Persia, Afghanistan, Kashmir, and the Himalayas east to Nepal, wintering in western and southern India. Still another one *(agricola)* breeds in northeastern India, and others in the Ryukyu Islands and Formosa. These oriental Turtle Doves thrive as aviary birds.

The AFRICAN TURTLE DOVE *(Streptopelia lugens)* is another closely allied species, only much duller and darker. It has rarely, if ever, been imported, as it is not very showy. It is found in Abyssinia, southern Arabia, central and eastern Africa, and on some plateaus in Nigeria and the Cameroon.

The MADAGASCAR TURTLE DOVE *(Streptopelia picturata)* is a large and fine species. It is distinguishable by its unmottled upper wing-coverts and absence of collar. Its head is gray; wings brown; scapulars vinaceous-purple; fore-neck and breast vinaceous, fading to white under the tail. The feathers of the back and the sides of the neck are black at the base, with bifurcated grayish-vinaceous tips, forming a slightly mottled patch; the lateral tail-feathers are dark gray with ashy tips. Numerous races live on the small islands about Madagascar. Though these sizeable doves are common, they keep to fairly well-wooded regions and plantations. To flourish in captivity, they need sufficient space; they are always rare in collections.

The Ring Doves consist of seven species, all characterized by a black ring around the back and sides of the neck, open in front. The well-known domestic Barbary Dove typifies the group.

The INDIAN RING DOVE *(Streptopelia decaocto)* haunts towns, villages, and cultivated grounds. It is very sociable. Its call, "coo-coo-coo," is quite different from that of the domestic bird, which it otherwise resembles completely, being only slightly darker. Its head, neck, and breast are pale vinous, lighter on the forehead and chin; flanks, belly and under tail coverts light gray; a black ring on the hindneck; back and scapulars pale brown, passing to pearl-gray on the wings; lateral tail-feathers black at the base and whitish-gray at the tip. This dove is found in Europe and has, in the last twenty years, spread west into France and Great Britain. It extends east to China and Japan, south to Palestine, Iraq, Persia, India, and Ceylon. It does nicely in captivity.

The BURMESE RING DOVE *(Streptopelia xanthocyclus)* is found in Burma, Yunnan, and southeastern China. It is somewhat larger and more brightly colored than the Indian bird, having a broad, yellow ring around the eyes instead of a bluish-gray one. It has occasionally been imported.

The AFRICAN RING DOVE *(Streptopelia roseogrisea)* is a little smaller and very much like the domestic dove, with the head, neck, and breast washed with delicate pink. It is common in the arid scrub of Lake Chad east to Darfur, the Sudan, and western Ethiopia. A race *(arabica)* with bluish-gray under-wing inhabits the Red Sea coasts of Africa and Arabia, while another one *(bornuensis)* extends west of the Chad to Timbuktu. It has seldom been kept in captivity.

The HALF-COLLARED RING DOVE *(Streptopelia semitorquata)* is the largest of the group. Its crown is gray, paler on forehead, and the cheeks have a buffy tinge. There is a large, black collar on the hind-neck; the remainder of the head, neck, and chest are deep vinaceous-pink, passing to lead-gray under the tail. The tail and wings are dark-brown; a red cere encircles the eyes. This dove lives all over Africa, with several other races, and feeds on grain, wild seeds, and berries on the edges of clearings. It is often imported and breeds well in captivity.

The DECEPTIVE RING DOVE *(Streptopelia decipiens)* is widespread in West and East Africa, having many local races. It is a small edition of the Half-collared, with a very broad, black collar edged above with ashy-white. It is a common species of the African savannas, nesting on acacia trees. Its curious note, sounding like "nurr," corresponds to the "laughing" of the domestic Barbary Dove. It is not often imported. It nests readily, but is not hardy.

Andamanese Cuckoo Dove *(Macropygia rufipennis)*, male on the right.

Bartlett's Pigeon *(Gallicolumba criniger)*. This species differs slightly from Bleeding Heart by its more extensive chest marking. A San Diego Zoo photo.

Note the incomplete ring on the neck of this Half-collared Ring Dove *(Streptopelia semitorquata)*. A New York Zoological Soceity photo.

The CAPE RING DOVE *(Streptopelia capicola)* inhabits East and South Africa; it is very common near Cape Town, both in pairs and in flocks. Its constant cooing is harsh. Its upper-parts are grayish-brown, changing to lead-gray on the wings. Rump and tail are brown, the outer rectrices black and white; crown lead-gray; sides of head, neck and breast vinaceous-gray; middle of the belly and vent white; a black collar and a black line running from bill to eye. The Cape race is the darkest. Throughout the range there are numerous others differing only in details. Though this dove flourishes in captivity, it is rarely kept.

The VINACEOUS RING DOVE *(Streptopelia vinacea)* is the smallest and brightest of the African Ring Doves. It is very common in the countryside from the Senegal to Abyssinia, south to the Cameroon and Uganda. It has several local races. Its call, the well-known "barbaru," is continually heard wherever this dove lives. Its head, neck, and underparts are vinaceaous-pink, whitish on the forehead, chin, throat, and below the tail; a black collar, edged with white above, and a black line from bill to eye; the upper-parts are earthy-brown, the bend of the wing gray; the lateral tail-feathers are black, with white tips. Being the prettiest of the African Ring Doves, it is often imported. It breeds easily.

The DOUBLE-COLLARED TURTLE DOVE *(Streptopelia bitorquata)* of Java and the Lesser Sunda Islands is a fine species, the size of a Barbary Dove. It is earthy-brown above, the wings having lead-gray patches, the lateral tail-feathers with gray tips; the crown is gray, paler in front; the chin whitish; the hind-neck vinaceous; a double black and pale gray collar appears on the hind-neck; the under-parts are vinaceous. This dove is not often imported, though it thrives in captivity, as do other Turtle Doves.

The PHILIPPINE TURTLE DOVE *(Streptopelia b. dussumieri)* is very similar, but lighter in color and without a vinaceous tinge on the hind neck. The nuchal collar is wide and black, followed by a band of pinkish-brown; the flanks are bluish-gray. This dove is common in the Philippines, but has seldom been kept in America or in Europe.

The DWARF TURTLE DOVE *(Streptopelia tranquebarica)* is a charming bird, the smallest of the Turtle Doves, and the only species of the genus in which male and female differ in color. It is Asiatic, breeding in Tibet and China, the northern Philippines and northern Indochina, wintering south of this range *(humilis)*; another race *(tranquebarica)*, slightly paler, nests in northern India, and an intermediate race *(murmensis)* in eastern Nepal, Sikkim, and Assam. It is a common, confiding species of the well-wooded countries, frequenting gardens. The male's head, lower back, rump, upper tail-coverts, under-wing and flanks are gray; his upper parts vinaceous-red; a black collar on the nape; the lateral tail-feathers are black, with pale gray tips. The female is a uniform earth-brown, with a black collar. These handsome doves, which live and nest well in aviaries, are often kept and bred.

The SPOTTED TURTLE DOVE *(Streptopelia chinensis)* is fairly different from the Ring Doves. Its various races range from India *(suratensis)* and Ceylon *(ceylonensis)* to China *(chinensis)*, Formosa *(formosa)*, Hainan *(hainana)*, Burma, Malaya, Indochina, Palawan, Borneo, and the Sunda Islands from Sumatra to Babar *(tigrina)*. They are very numerous in both cultivated and open country, coming close to houses and feeding in fields and yards.

Some people who are not familiar with the characteristics of a Bleeding Heart Pigeon think that the red spot is really a wound. Photo by A.J. Mobbs.

By nature a forest-dwelling bird, a Bleeding Heart Pigeon in captivity will build a nest above the ground on trees or bushes. Photo by A.J. Mobbs.

Streptopelia chinensis tigrina found in the area of Burma and malaya. It is intermediate between the Indian and Chinese forms of the species *S. chinensis*. A New York Zoological Society photo.

Their tail is fairly long; head gray; nape and sides of neck black, dotted with white spots; upper-parts brown; outer wing-coverts gray; under-parts vinous; three outer-feathers broadly tipped with white. The race *tigrina* is smaller, with its under tail-coverts white, and dark shafts in the wing-coverts. The Indian race *(suratensis)* has the wing-coverts marked with two reddish dots near the tip, producing a spotted effect. It is the most attractive form. Spotted Turtle Doves are commonly kept. Moreover, they have been acclimatized in many parts of the world, particularly in Los Angeles, Calif., where they abound in gardens.

The PALM TURTLE DOVES *(Streptopelia senegalensis)*, together with their local races, occupy the whole of Africa, from Morocco, Algeria, and Egypt to the Cape Colony, extending to Arabia, Palestine, Syria, east to India and Turkestan. Their head and breast are a rich vinous; a spotted black-and-rusty collar appears on the front and the sides of the neck; the upper-parts are brown, the feathers marked with vinous; the lower back, rump, wing-coverts, and secondaries are bluish-gray; the lower belly and the vent are white. The Indian race *(cambayensis)* has the upper-parts, including the rump, a plain earth-brown. These attractive doves are very common in villages and gardens throughout their range. They are pretty, tame, and familiar. The Senegal Palm Dove is commonly imported, kept, and bred in captivity, as is the Indian race. These birds stay well at liberty in gardens, and they are very prolific.

CUCKOO DOVES

A well-marked genus *(Macropygia)* contains most of the Cuckoo Doves which are characterized by a small bill, long wings, a very long tail, and short legs. Although coming often to the ground to feed on seeds and fallen berries, they walk with some difficulty and are mainly arboreal. Their plumage is brown or chestnut, often remarkably barred and metallic. Quiet and tame by nature, they inhabit glades and open parts of the forest. They live in the Oriental and Australian regions, south to Australia. Being wood doves, they are not easily seen. Although they do well and breed in captivity, they are seldom imported. They are very quiet, harmless to other birds, and several pairs can be kept together in a large flight.

The BAR-TAILED CUCKOO DOVE *(Macropygia unchall)*, with three closely similar races, is found from Kashmir and Szechuan to Hainan, Fokhien and Annam, *(tusalia, minor)* and also in Malaya, Sumatra, Java, and Lombock *(unchall)* in mountain forests. It occurs above 3,000 feet, and one can now and then see small groups perching motionless on trees, coming at intervals to the ground to feed in clearings. They fly with a loud wing-clapping, but never far. Their coo is deep and ends in a sort of gurgle. They usually lay one egg per clutch, although I found two eggs in a nest in central Indochina. They are never numerous at any given spot, but widely distributed, and not rare. Top and sides of the male's head grayish-buff, strongly tinged with metallic green and lilac, the nape amethyst; the upper-parts are blackish-brown, barred with chestnut, including the tail, the outer pairs of feathers tipped with gray; chin and throat pinkish-buff; breast of the same color, with amethyst reflections; belly is buff, passing to

Wonga-wonga Pigeon *(Leucosarcia melanoleuca).* The markings and colors of this eastern Australian pigeon blend so well with tree stumps in the wild that hunters find them hard to see. Photo by K. Hindwood.

The black bars on the wings and silvery gray color are characteristic of pigeons descended from the Rock Pigeon *(Columba livia).* A CLI photo.

cinnamon below the tail. The female differs in having the head and under-parts barred with blackish-brown. These beautiful doves are large and very striking, both in shape and in color; the metallic reflections of the plumage are very vivid. They have always been rare in captivity: the London Zoo long ago received a few specimens of the Malaysian race. I brought over six pairs *(minor)* from Laos in 1926, giving some to Mme. Lecallier and Mr. A. Ezra. They bred in their aviaries, also at Cleres in 1926 and 1927, and every year since, one egg per clutch being laid in all cases. They proved to be steady, although slow, breeders. Eventually some of their offspring found their way to California, where the species was well established until 1940, but it disappeared during the last war. There are none at present in captivity.

The AMBOINA CUCKOO DOVE *(Macropygia amboinensis)*, in the form of many races, is found in the Moluccas, New Guinea, and neighboring islands. It is chestnut-brown above, the nape and upper mantle having brilliant green and purple reflections; the breast is vinaceous, shot with purple and barred with black. In the hen, the upper-parts are brown, barred with chestnut. The New Guinea race *(doreya)* has been imported extensively.

The RED-HEADED CUCKOO DOVE *(Macropygia ruficeps)* is much smaller, chestnut-red, dark above, light below, the feathers tipped with fulvous-white on the breast; the sides of neck and mantle have lilac reflections. The hen is duller, with no reflections; the breast feathers are barred black and red, and those of the back are tipped with pale brown. It inhabits Burma, Indochina, and Malaysia, east to the Lesser Sunda Islands. I brought a few specimens from Indochina, which failed to breed. It is a pretty little dove, no larger than the Zebra Dove.

The PHEASANT-TAILED CUCKOO DOVE *(Macropygia phasianella)* is approximately the size of a Bar-tailed Dove and is represented by many local races in Borneo, the Philippines, Malaysia, and Australia. The Malaysian subspecies *(emiliana)* once came to the London Zoo. It is dark brown mottled with chestnut above; its tail is rufescent, cinnamon below. There are lilac reflections on the nape, neck, back and breast. The female has the hind-neck barred with black.

The Philippine subspecies *(tenuirostris)* is similar, but somewhat more slender. Imported into California during the last twenty

94

Bar-tailed Cuckoo Dove *(Macropygia unchall)*. A very long tail is a feature common to the members of *Macropygia*, which literally means big tail. A New York Zoological Society photo.

Shown are two of the many varieties of domestic pigeons bred to-day. Understandably, highly selected breeds can survive only in captivity. Photos by L. van der Meid.

Through artificial selection breeders can develop almost any part of the anatomy, like the feather ornaments on the legs. Photo from *Encyclopedia of Pigeon Breeds*.

years, it nested successfully in my aviaries recently. One of the New Guinea subspecies has figured also at the London Zoo. It is darker, richer, more metallic in color. The Australian subspecies *(phasianella)*, which is quite similar, has seldom appeared in captivity.

Among other species, all chestnut, and varying in size are: *magna* (Celebes and nearby islands); *rufipennis* (Andamans and Nicobar Islands); *nigrirostris* (New Guinea), and *mackinlayi* (New Hebrides, Solomons, and other islands), which to my knowledge have not yet been kept in aviaries.

Three other genera of the same group—large, striking, and beautiful—have reached neither America nor Europe alive: *Turacoena*, with two slaty-black species, one with white forehead and cheeks, found in the Celebes and neighboring islands; *Rheinwardtoena*, containing also two fine species: very large, long-tailed, pale gray on head, neck, and under-parts, and chestnut or black above. They live in the Moluccas, New Guinea, and adjoining islands. Lastly, *Coryphoenas* from the Solomons: very long-tailed, slaty-gray, with brown crest and large, red bill. All these attractive doves would make desirable additions to any collection.

A typical construction of perches for domestic homing pigeons. Each unit is called a "pigeonhole," a term with many meanings in the English language apart from its literal meaning of the perch or living quarters of a pigeon. Photo by L. van der Meid.

It is reported that the Pheasant-tailed Cuckoo Dove *(Macropygia phasianella)* uses the tail as support when feeding in shrubs and trees. Photo by Elvie.

AFRICAN WOOD DOVES

A small genus *(Aplopelia)* of two species inhabits the woods of Africa, keeping to the dense bush and usually seen feeding on the ground on berries. They nest in low creepers.

The RUFOUS-NECKED WOOD DOVE *(Aplopelia larvata)* is resident in the highlands of Abyssinia *(bronzina)* and of East and South Africa *(larvata)*. Its upper-parts are olive-brown, the upper back slate-gray, with copper-green edges to the feathers; outer tail-feathers tipped gray; the front of the head is white, the back of head and neck coppery purple; foreneck and breast vinous, passing on the belly to cinnamon. The hen is slightly smaller and duller. This handsome dove has been imported. It has often been bred in captivity, particularly at Cleres, France.

The subspecies *(Aplopelia l. simplex)* occurs in Uganda, the Cameroons, and the islands off the coast, and has never been imported. It is darker above, pale below, less metallic on the neck, and its forehead is gray.

Yellow-eyed Stock Pigeon *(Columba eversmanni)*. Because this bird is very close to the common European Stock Pigeon, some authors consider it as a form of *C. oenas.*

Snow Pigeon *(Columba leuconota)*. The white neck and breast are easy to recognize even during flight.

American Quail Pigeons and Doves

In the tropical parts of the Americas certain doves or pigeons live mainly on the ground. Their legs and beaks are comparatively long, their tails short. In appearance and behavior, they suggest partridges and quails.

Though their wings always lack metallic spots, they usually show rich green and purple reflections on neck and mantle. Several species are beautiful and make excellent aviary birds. Since most of them are delicate, they require shelter and heat in frosty weather. During the day they stay mostly on the ground. Their food consists of seed and berries, also grubs, worms, and insects. In captivity, they should have animal food, especially when nesting, such as raw meat, soaked biscuit, cheese, mockingbird food, mealworms and earthworms, which aid them in rearing their young successfully. These doves are usually quiet and fairly sociable with other species.

The genus *Leptotila* is represented by many species and subspecies from Mexico to Argentina. Although living principally on the ground, they are not so specialized as the other genera of the group. Most of them frequent woods and forests, but some *(L. verreauxi)* are found in savannas, cultivated fields, and meadows. I remember seeing hundreds perched on the fences of cattle ranches in the interior of Venezuela. With few exceptions, they are dully-colored, hence not popular as aviary birds, although they live and breed well in captivity.

VERREAUX'S GROUND DOVES *(Leptotila verreauxi)* are found under several races throughout Mexico, Central and South America, south to Argentina, Bolivia, and Peru. They inhabit forests, second-growth woods, cultivated country, and savannas, according to localities. Their coloration is grayish-brown above, the nape and hind-neck with coppery and green reflections. Forehead, throat, breast, and sides pale vinous; under-wings and quills partly chestnut. Now and then, they have been kept in aviaries, especially at the London Zoo in 1907, and Mell Strann, California dove enthusiast, has reared many in recent years. This dove is rather sluggish and therefore not in keen demand.

The subspecies *chalchauchenia*, from Argentina and neighboring countries, with whitish forehead and white belly, was raised in England by the late Miss Alderson.

The GRAY-CROWNED GROUND DOVE *(Leptotila plumbeiceps)* occurs from southern Mexico to Colombia. It is plain olive-brown above; its forehead is pale gray; crown, nape, hind-neck, and mantle slightly glossed with purple; cheeks, throat, and under-parts vinaceous-buff, passing to white on the vent; wings have cinnamon patches. Occasionally this very plain bird has been imported, sometimes in large numbers. It bred in 1912 and 1913 in my aviaries at Villers-Bretonneux.

The GRAY-FRONTED GROUND DOVE *(Leptotila rufaxilla)* resembles the Gray-crowned, which it replaces southward to Brazil. Its plumage is olive above, with lilac reflections. It is common in Guiana, in cane and rice fields, in the savannas and in second-growth jungle. During floods, these doves congregate on higher ground. They nest on small bushes and trees, sometimes on the roots of trees. They are seldom imported. The subspecies *reichenbachi*, from southeastern Brazil and Uruguay, has the chin and middle of the throat white; cheeks, sides of neck and flanks deep reddish-vinous. The late Miss Alderson, well-known British dove fancier, bred this species.

The WHITE-FRONTED GROUND DOVE *(Leptotila jamaicensis)* also called Amethyst Dove, is by far the prettiest of the genus. It inhabits Jamaica, there being other races in Grand Cayman and St. Andrews Islands. This attractive dove feeds on the ground in woods and is said to like orange pips. It nests very low, sometimes on logs. It is olive brown above and has a white forehead and a gray crown; its back and the sides of its neck are metallic pink, with golden or blue-green reflections; its cheeks, throat and under-parts are white. The hen is not quite so brightly colored. This is a charming species to keep, and it breeds well.

Eastern Rock Pigeon *(Columba rupestris)*. The species is found in Central and eastern Asia.

Eastern Wood Pigeon *(Columba palumbus casiotis)*, a northern Indian race of Wood Pigeon.

Miss Alderson raised it for the first time in 1903. A few are produced each year in various California aviaries.

The GRENADA GROUND DOVE *(Leptotila wellsi)* is brown above; its forehead is pinkish-white; its crown gray; its chin and throat are white, passing to vinous on the breast; its abdomen and under-tail are cinnamon. A rather attractive species, it found its way occasionally to England, where H. Bright raised young in 1926.

CASSIN'S GROUND DOVE *(Leptotila cassini)*, from Central America and northern Colombia, is a dark species, olive-brown with gray crown and hind-neck; the chin and center of throat are white; under-parts gray, and under tail-coverts brown. It has been represented in several collections, including my own. There is no record of it having been bred.

Two other species—*L. megalura*, from Bolivia, and *L. ochraceiventris*, from Ecuador, have never been imported.

The Quail Doves, or American Ground Pigeons *(Geotrygon)* are larger, heavier, long-legged. Though definitely adapted to a terrestrial life, they roost and nest in trees. They are found in Mexico and Cuba, extending to southern Brazil, in many fine species. In captivity they thrive and breed freely, provided they are kept frost-free and given much animal food. Usually they are good-tempered and tame. Their clutch consists of two fawn-colored eggs.

The CRESTED QUAIL DOVE, MOUNTAIN WITCH *(Geotrygon versicolor)* is a most beautiful bird. As large as a European gray partridge, it lives in the deepest glades of the most hidden mountains of the island of Jamaica, where at present it is very rare. It walks about on the forest ground; when disturbed, it tries to escape on foot. At each step it jerks its tail up and down. The Mountain Witch nests on low trees or on their exposed roots. Its name is derived from its call, which is deep and sounds like a distant groan.

These ground pigeons have their occiput and nape feathers long, forming a thick occipital crest. Their forehead and crest are olive-gray, a broad, reddish-buff streak marking the cheeks; the neck is golden-green, shot with purple, the throat rufous-buff; the mantle purplish-chestnut; the lower back, rump, and tail-coverts are a greenish-blue, with a purple gloss; the primaries cinnamon, the secondaries and tail blackish-green; the under-parts are pale vinous; the flanks and under-tail chestnut. The hens are a little smaller and duller, but difficult to sex.

The London Zoo received specimens at intervals from 1860 on and bred this species in 1904. Some twenty years ago, the Mountain Witch was imported into California and bred successfully by Carl Naether and other aviculturists, who sent some to Europe. In fact, Mr. Naether's original pair has been producing young for eleven successive years. My pairs at Cleres bred successfully, as did those kept in England. There are now many pairs in captivity which raise young each season.

A Gray-headed Quail Dove (Geotrygon caniceps) perched near its nest, a wicker basket. Photo by L. van der Meid.

The GRAY-HEADED QUAIL DOVE *(Geotrygon caniceps)* from Cuba, also very rare and beautiful, is a little smaller. It has no crest. The destruction of the thick, low-altitude forests has wiped out this very handsome bird in most of its former range. It has a whitish forehead, changing to gray on the crown; the neck is gray, with green and violet reflections; the mantle glossy violet, passing to dark blue on the rump; the wings are grayish-brown with a metallic gloss; the throat is whitish; the breast gray, and the under-tail cinnamon. This fine species was brought to France, where Mme. Lecallier reared it in 1923, and to England, where Mr. Ezra bred it in 1925. There are now very few in captivity. A slightly different subspecies, with a pure white forehead, *leucometopius,* found in San Domingo, has not been kept in captivity.

Andamanese Wood Pigeon *(Columba palumboides)* is limited to the Andaman and Nicobar Islands.

Hodgson's Wood Pigeon *(Columba hodgsoni)*.

The GOLDEN or KEY-WEST QUAIL DOVE *(Geotrygon chrysia)* is common in the rocky and wooded regions of Cuba, where it forages for seeds, berries and grubs among dead leaves. It inhabits also Haiti, the Bahamas, and occasionally the Florida Keys. Its coloration is as follows: forehead brownish-red, changing into metallic green on crown and nape; upper-parts reddish-cinnamon, the feathers edged with brilliant metallic purple, more golden on lower back and rump; a white stripe runs from the bill to the ear-coverts; the lower parts are grayish-white, with a vinous tinge on the lower throat and breast. The female is somewhat duller colored, less metallic. Occasionally these beautiful Quail Doves have found their way into the London Zoo. Mr. Astley, well-known British bird fancier, had one in 1908. It was reared in Paris in 1870. In 1923 and thereafter, large numbers came to France. They are easy to keep. Mme. Lecallier and Mr. Decoux raised some. On the whole, these doves do not nest readily in captivity. At present there seems to be only a few either in American or in European collections.

The MOUSTACHE QUAIL DOVE *(Geotrygon mystacea)*, from the Lesser West Indies, is similar, but browner, less reddish, with rich-green instead of purple reflections on head, neck, and mantle. The white stripe across the face is broader and accentuated by a dark brown one below. These doves are still reasonably numerous in the undisturbed forests of Guadeloupe, Desirade, Montserrat, and some other islands, but they have become rare in Martinique. They are quite insectivorous. Although the noted German ornithologist Russ possessed this dove long ago, there is no accurate old record of its having been bred in captivity. At present a few pairs are in the United States, including two in my collection. After four years, one pair has reared young in a large aviary where they are associated with a number of other doves.

The MARTINIQUE QUAIL DOVE *(Geotrygon martinicana)* also inhabits the Lesser West Indies in mountain forests, where it runs so fast that it is difficult to approach. Trapping and shooting have reduced its numbers as has the introduced mongoose. Although somewhat shorter, it is almost as large as the preceding species. The male is bright chestnut, with brilliant purple reflections above, notably on the hind-neck and back; his forehead is

Moustache Quail Dove *(Geotrygon mystacea)*. It is quite obvious from what feature this species gets its popular name. Photo by Elvie.

pinkish-fawn; there is a vinous-chestnut patch on the ear-coverts, a buff stripe on the face, from bill to ear-coverts, and white, vertical bar on the sides of the breast, just before the wings; the under-parts are ochraceous-cinnamon, paler on the throat and under the tail. The hen is quite different: plain brown above, cinnamon-buff below, without markings or metallic reflections. The Martinique Quail Dove thrives in captivity. The few specimens now in the United States include several in my aviaries, where one pair raised six young in 1954, and more since then.

The RUDDY QUAIL DOVE *(Geotrygon montana)* is the most widely-known and commonest of the genus, both at liberty and in captivity. A typical ground pigeon, it nests on saplings and small trees fairly low in the forests, ranging from the Greater West Indies and southern Mexico to Brazil, Paraguay, Bolivia, and Peru. It looks like the Martinique Quail Dove, except that both sexes are much smaller and lighter colored. It has been kept in captivity for many years, where it breeds well, rearing brood after brood if given sufficient animal food. It nested first in the London Zoo in 1863.

Ashy Wood Pigeon *(Columba pulchricollis).*

Purple Wood Pigeon *(Columba punicea).*

Chiriqui Quail Dove *(Geotrygon chiriquensis).* Photo by Elvie.

The CHIRIQUI QUAIL DOVE *(Geotrygon chiriquensis)* is found in Costa Rica's mountain forests. It is a large, high-legged, short-bodied pigeon. Its coloring is chestnut above, rufous below; the crown and nape are gray, the face pale fulvous, with a dark brown line running from beak to ear-coverts. Both sexes look alike, except that the hen is slightly smaller and duller. The pair I obtained in Costa Rica in January of 1953 began to nest at my Los Angeles aviaries in January of 1955, and by April they had already reared three pairs of young. They raise regularly from five to six pairs a year. The offspring, however, laid only infertile eggs in both M. Strann's and Carl Naether's aviaries, despite excellent feeding and care.

The WHITE-FACED QUAIL DOVE *(Geotrygon albifacies),* from southern Mexico and Central America, is very similar except for its white forehead and the black lines formed by the bases of feathers on the sides of the neck. This dove has been raised in California.

The VENEZUELAN QUAIL DOVE *(Geotrygon linearis)* closely resembles the Chiriqui, but its mantle is purplish-blue; its crown rufous, bounded on both sides by gray; the sides of the head are whitish, the throat white and also the center of the belly. The London Zoo had this dove in 1909. Other races live in Colombia and Trinidad.

Other South American species approximate more or less the Chiriqui Quail Doves, but differ in details of color *(G. erythropareia, G. bourcieri, G. violacea)*, while others from Central America, have a white face with two black stripes *(G. lawrencei, G. goldmani, G. costaricensis, G. veraguensis)*. None of these handsome birds have found their way into either American or European aviaries. *G. saphirina*, a beautiful ground pigeon from the Andes of Colombia, Ecuador, and Peru, also has never been imported. It is purplish-chestnut above, white and vinous below; with the forehead, sides of head, and throat pure white; a black stripe runs from bill to ear-coverts; the crown and nape are black; the hind-neck is golden-green.

The BLUE-HEADED QUAIL DOVE *(Staroenas cyanocephala)* used to be common in the forests of Cuba's rocky districts. It is somewhat longer in shape than the *Geotrygon;* it carries the tail slightly upward. It walks slowly on the ground in search of seeds, berries, and grubs. It roosts on low branches and nests on top of vines and parasitic plants, laying two round, white eggs. Blue-headed Quail Doves have been sharply reduced in numbers by deforestation and excessive hunting. They are strikingly beautiful, the sexes being alike: the crown is rich cobalt-blue, bordered by a black line running through the eyes; the upper-parts are olive-brown; there is a broad, white band running up from the chin, below the eyes, to the back of the head; the throat and upper-breast are black, bordered below by a semicircular white stripe; the front and sides of the black area are tipped with blue; the remaining plumage is plain rust-colored. This lovely dove has been popular since the 18th century. It was bred first in 1870 at the London Zoo. Since then it has been repeatedly reared in America and in Europe. Being quiet and sociable, the Blue-headed Quail Dove is a highly satisfactory aviary bird. It must be sheltered from frost and be fed some soft food.

White-crowned Pigeon *(Columba leucocephala)*. Photo by A.J. Mobbs.

Band-tailed Pigeon *(Columba fasciata)*. The parti-colored bill is characteristic of North American forms. A San Diego Zoo photo.

Nicobar Pigeon *(Caloenas nicobarica)*. The hackles or neck feathers are more prominent in the male than in the female. Photo by Dr. Herbert R. Axelrod.

Pacific Ground Pigeons

From the islands off Southeast Asia and the Pacific come certain doves and pigeons which, like their American cousins, feed on the ground and walk with the greatest ease, but roost at night and nest on trees and bushes. The smallest, varying from the size of a Mourning Dove to that of a partridge, belong to the large genus *Gallicolumba,* found in the Philippines, New Guinea, and many islands of Melanesia, Micronesia, and Polynesia. A larger genus, *Leucosarcia,* inhabits Australia; another, *Trugon,* New Guinea.

The very large and beautiful *Otidiphaps,* from the New Guinea area; the Nicobar Pigeon, found on small islets from the Gulf of Bengal to the Philippines, New Guinea, and the Solomons; the very rare, probably extinct *Microgura,* confined to Choiseul Island; and the huge Crown Pigeons *(Goura)* proper to New Guinea and vicinity, although related to the present group, will be discussed in a special chapter, as will the thick-billed, very peculiar Samoan Pigeon *(Didunculus).*

All these ground pigeons have long, fleshy legs, usually crimson. They feed on seeds, berries, worms, and insects. They thrive in captivity; but since most species are susceptible to cold, they should be sheltered during the winter in cold regions. While many are fairly sociable and harmless to other birds, a few are very quarrelsome.

The BLEEDING HEART PIGEON *(Gallicolumba luzonica)* is a wonder of the avian world. Anyone interested in birds knows these strange-looking doves with a perfect imitation of a bleeding wound on their white breasts. They are found on forest floors in the Philippine Island of Luzon, where they walk about and feed on berries and grubs. Their coloration is not only odd, but very attractive: the forehead is whitish, passing to gray on the crown; the back is purplish-maroon; the upper-parts are grayish-brown, glossed with brilliant metallic green. The wing-coverts have broad,

Above:
A Bleeding Heart
Pigeon *(Gallicolumba
luzonica)* seen from
the back and front.
Photos by Elvie.
Right:
Bartlett's Pigeon
*(Gallicolumba
criniger)* is closely
related to the Bleed-
ing Heart, but it is
more colorful. Photo
by L. van der Meid.

Blue Crowned Pigeon *(Goura cristata)*. Photo by Dr. Herbert R. Axelrod at the San Diego Zoo.

The colors of a bird, iridescent birds in particular, in photographs are affected by lighting conditions. Note the striking difference in the color of this Blue Crowned Pigeon and the one on the facing page. Photo courtesy of Vogelpark Walsrode.

reddish-brown and bluish-gray bars; the under-parts are white, tinged with buffy salmon on the sides. On the center of the breast appears a patch of blood-red, stiff feathers—the "bleeding heart." The female is very much like the male, but a little smaller and duller, with a thinner bill and a smaller head. Her under-parts show more buff. These pigeons are often difficult to sex, because, though many hens have a less vivid and smaller red breast patch, others have it as bright and as large as any male.

Bleeding Heart Pigeons are much sought after as aviary birds. They bred first in the London Zoo in 1887, and soon after in many public and private collections, first in Europe, later in America. They will nest in boxes or baskets hung on the wall, never on the ground. If they get sufficient soft food, they will raise their squabs readily. They are usually peaceful with other doves, but there are exceptions. In captivity they become tame and live well provided they are kept reasonably warm in winter.

BARTLETT'S PIGEON (*Gallicolumba criniger*) takes the place of the Bleeding Heart in Mindanao, where it is rather uncommon and local in dry, lowland forests. Though a near-relative of the Bleeding Heart, this beautiful species is quite different in coloration. Its head, neck, and mantle are greener; the back and wings are rich chestnut, with green and purple reflections, the chin and throat are white, which color descends in a narrow line on each side of the breast, dividing the green sides from an extensive crimson-maroon patch on the breast, which is much larger and more uniform in color than in the Bleeding Heart, also harsher and stiffer in texture. The remaining under-parts are a rich fawn.

Bartlett's Pigeons are well known, if rare, in captivity, where they behave like Bleeding Hearts. The London Zoo had them in 1863 and bred them in 1864, actually long before *luzonica*. Mr. Newman raised one in 1907, and Mme. Lecallier and others raised some between 1920 and 1930. Mr. Ezra reared hybrids between *luzonica* and *criniger*. At present some pairs are in the United States and breeding. Whereas the Bleeding Hearts lay two eggs, the Bartlett Pigeons lay only one in each clutch.

Allied species and subspecies inhabit other Philippine islands, differing mainly in the size of the red breast patch and the intensity of the green on the upper-parts: *platenae* (Mindoro); *keayi* (Negros) with a very small red patch, which has been in the

Steinbeck, Calif., collection; *leytensis* (Leyte and Samar); *basilanica* (Basilan), which resembles *criniger; menagei* (Tawi-Tawi). All would be desirable additions to our collections.

The GOLDEN HEART PIGEON *(Gallicolumba rufigula)*, of New Guinea and neighboring islands, is smaller and redder than the Philippine species, but resembles them in shape, color pattern and habits. It is found commonly in forests, being very wild and taking flight at the least alarm. It nests just off the ground and, so far as is known, lays a single, creamy-white egg. It has a buff forehead, the upper-parts vinous-chestnut; nape, neck, and upper back grayish, the wings with gray bars. A fairly distinct gray band runs from above the eyes to the occiput; the cheeks are pale vinous; the under-parts yellowish-white with a deep yellow patch of stiff feathers on the center of the breast; the flanks and under-tail are deep buff. This attractive species, which first came to the London Zoo in 1915, has since been imported by several aviculturists. I had some at Cleres, and Mr. Ezra reared one or two at Foxwarren between 1930 and 1940.

The following species of *Gallicolumba* lack the patch on the breast, which, however, is always white or lightcolored in contrast to the remainder of the plumage. Not all have been imported alive and kept in captivity. This is true of a rare species from Celebes, *G. tristigmata,* which is gray and brown, with much metallic green, and violet reflections above, contrasted by a pale yellow breast.

BECCARI'S GROUND PIGEON *(Gallicolumba beccarii)*, from the Solomon Islands and New Guinea, has many different races. The fore-part of its head, neck, throat, and breast are gray, the latter bordered by pale gray; smaller wing-coverts and a band below the gray breast are metallic purple; the upper-parts are dark olive; the under-parts grayish-brown. This pigeon, which is very rare in captivity, has been kept by Dr. E.W. Gifford of Oakland, Calif. quite some years ago.

In the same region are found three allied species: *G. solomonis* (S. Christobal); *G. sanctacrucis* (Santa Cruz Archipelago); and *G. canifrons* (Palau). All are not yet imported.

STAIR'S GROUND PIGEON *(Gallicolumba stairi)*, from Samoa, Fiji, and Tonga Islands, has vinous-rufous forehead, sides of head and neck, and breast, which turns white on the chin and

Sclater's Crowned Pigeon *(Goura scheepmakeri)*. It is obvious why this species is also called the Maroon-breasted Crowned Pigeon. A San Diego Zoo photo.

The crest of Sclater's Crowned Pigeon is longer and more lacy than that of the Blue Crowned Pigeon. Photo by Dr. Herbert R. Axelrod.

around the breast, which in turn is bordered behind by a deep-maroon band. The back of the head and neck are slate-colored, shot with green; the remaining upper-parts are glossy brown, with bronze and purple reflections; the remainder of the under-surface is dark brown. The female is smaller and has a pale chocolate-brown breast. Like all other species of the genus, this pigeon feeds on the ground. Often one finds it on the forest floor, taking wing at the slightest disturbance and gliding rapidly through the underbrush. It nests on low bushes, where it lays two white eggs. As early as 1883 the London Zoo exhibited this rare pigeon, which was bred by Dr. Gifford.

The BUFF-HOODED GROUND PIGEON *(Gallicolumba xanthonura),* from the Mariana, Caroline, and Yap Islands, has differently colored sexes. The male's crown, nape, and hind-neck are rusty rufous; the remaining upper-parts are dark bronzy olive; the feathers of the mantle and the wing coverts are bordered with purplish-violet; the forehead, anterior part of the face and breast buffy-white; the rest of the under-parts are brownish-black. The female has the upper-parts of the head cinnamon; the back has an olive luster, and the upper wing-coverts have rufous edges; the under-parts more rufous. This rare and handsome species had been kept by Dr. Gifford in Oakland, Calif. and by various Japanese aviculturists, in whose aviaries I saw it.

The WHITE-FRONTED GROUND PIGEON *(Gallicolumba kubaryi),* from Ruk and Ponape (Eastern Carolines), resembles the better-known Jobi Pigeon, which follows, differing in having the back of the head and nape slaty-gray, the purple of the mantle even more brilliant, and the anterior part of the head white. Dr. Gifford and Japanese dove fanciers have kept this very attractive pigeon.

The JOBI GROUND PIGEON *(Gallicolumba jobiensis),* common in New Guinea and neighboring islands, has a slightly different race inhabiting the Solomon islands of Guadalcanal and Vella Lavella. It is slaty-black, with the mantle amethyst-purple; the lores, sides of the forehead, superciliary stripes, throat, and breast are pure white. The sexes are difficult to distinguish; the females, however, are somewhat smaller and usually show less pure and bright colors. Imported into Europe and America after the first World War, this pigeon bred abundantly in England, France, and elsewhere. It is prolific, but dangerous to weaker species. In a spacious aviary many pairs will breed successfully, as has been the case for many years at Cleres. This pigeon is hardy despite its tropical origin. Even in cold countries, it is inclined to nest in winter. Though rare at present, it is one of the most desirable species in captivity.

The TUAMOTU GROUND PIGEON *(Gallicolumba erythroptera),* also found in the Society Islands, resembles *jobiensis* and *kubaryi,* but has more white on the head. It has not been imported yet.

The GRAY-HOODED GROUND PIGEON *(Gallicolumba rubescens),* from the Marquesas, is smaller. Until 1920 it was known only from an old plate published in 1814. The Whitney Expedition, which rediscovered the species in 1923, sent 31 live specimens to Dr. Gifford, who raised many youngsters. Some were sent to England and to France, where Mme. Lecallier raised some during the following years. These curious little doves are extremely quarrelsome and vicious, fighting constantly, even mates of the same pair, the male bullying the hen, sometimes even killing her. This bad temper has caused this once well-established species gradually to disappear from aviaries, the last specimens in California having died about 1945. These doves have the head, neck, and breast gray; the remaining plumage fuscous-black; the back, scapulars, lesser and long coverts broadly margined with metallic violet-purple and the primaries and rectrices with a white base. The female is duller.

The small island of Wetar, near Timor, is the home of a fine species—*Gallicolumba hoedtia.* It has a gray head; the throat, sides of the neck and upper-breast are white; the upper-parts coppery reddish, with a violet gloss; the under-parts are brownish-black. This species has not been imported.

The WONGA-WONGA PIGEON *(Leucosarcia melanoleuca)* represents the group in Australia. It is very different from all the other species in that it is as large as a domestic pigeon, but has a short tail and high legs. Its upper-parts are leaden-gray; the forehead and chin are white; there is a white line under the eye to the ear-coverts; the cheeks are pale gray; neck and breast leaden-gray, the latter divided by a broad, semicircular white belt; the remaining under-parts are white, the feathers of the flanks and abdomen having black, triangular spots. This fine pigeon inhabits

Victoria Crowned Pigeon *(Goura victoria).* Its crest is very distinctive: dark blue, with the flattened ends tipped with white. Photo by A.J. Mobbs.

Gouras are closely related and they have similar nesting habits.
Nests are built off the ground as shown at the San Diego Zoo with
one of the crowned pigeons in it. Photo by Dr. H.R. Axelrod.

eastern Australia (Queensland, New South Wales, and Victoria). It is fairly common in the Blue Mountains, in wooded country. The Wonga-wonga Pigeon walks on the ground, feeding on berries and seeds. When startled, it rises with a loud clapping of the wings to perch in a tree, where it will remain on a horizontal branch in scrub forest, ten to twenty feet off the ground. It lays two pure white eggs. The Wonga-wonga has been kept and reared in captivity. Its large size and handsome pied plumage make it attractive, although its monotonous, high-pitched, endlessly repeated coo—"hoo, hoo, hoo . . .," which can be heard a half a mile away, is decidedly tiresome. It is not only hardy and a ready nester, but also harmless to other species.

A beautiful species, not yet imported, *Trugon terrestris,* is found in New Guinea and nearby islands. Its head, foreneck, upperback, and breast are bluish gray; the cheeks paler and the forehead brownish; the sides and back of the neck are blackish; the remainder of the upper-parts olive gray; the belly creamy-buff; the sides bright rufous. This species is only a little smaller than the Wonga-wonga; it lives on the forest floor.

Rock and Wood Pigeons

This group includes all large pigeons resembling the well-known Rock Pigeon, the ancestor of the domestic breeds, as well as the familiar European Wood Pigeon and the American Band-tailed Pigeon. They are large birds with fairly short legs, long wings, and moderately long tails. Many have metallic reflections on the neck and other parts of the body.

These pigeons are principally found on high trees or rocky cliffs, but many feed on the ground, where they walk with ease. A few species, however, eat berries off trees and seldom come to the ground. Their food consists of grain, seeds, beechnuts, acorns, berries, wild fruit, buds and leaves; also a certain amount of animal food, such as caterpillars, grubs, and worms. In captivity, a good mixture of wheat, corn (maize), peas, sorghum, and other seeds usually keeps them in good health, with the occasional addition of some dog-biscuits and green food. These large pigeons require plenty of room, as they have long wings and fly powerfully; their aviaries should be very spacious and high. Otherwise, they are likely to injure themselves on the wire partitions and lack sufficient exercise. They are usually harmless to other pigeons and doves. With the exception of the European species, the North American Band-tailed and the African Guinea Pigeons, they are not often kept by amateur aviculturists, although all species live well in captiviy and many are inclined to breed in confinement

Practically all these pigeons are placed in the genus *Columba*, as they are fairly similar, with many intermediates between the more differentiated forms. They are found throughout the world.

OLD WORLD PIGEONS

The Old World species are either Rock or Wood Pigeons, more or less equal in numbers.

THE GREEN IMPERIAL PIGEON—*CARPOPHAGA O OENEA*

Green Imperial Pigeon *(Ducula aenea).*

Opposite:
Mountain Imperial Pigeon
(Ducula badia).

The Stock Pigeon *(Columba oenas)* is widely distributed in Europe and also found in Africa and Eastern Asia. A Die Gefiederte Welt photo.

The ROCK PIGEON *(Columba livia)* is the well-known bird of the European rocky coasts and hills, also found in Asia and northern Africa. It has taken readily to nesting and dwelling on town buildings in various parts of the world. It is the ancestor of all domestic and feral breeds. It resembles the blue phase of the domestic pigeon, the many subspecies differing in depth of color, and in the white or gray on the rump.

A paler species, with white in the tail, occurs widely in central Asia *(C. rupestris)*.

The STOCK PIGEON *(C. oenas)* is another common European bird which lives on trees, nesting in holes. It is leaden-gray, with irregular black bars on the wings; the tail has a broad apical black band, the throat and crop region is purplish-vinous, the back and sides of the neck metallic green. This pigeon lives in Europe and in central Asia.

The SNOW PIGEON *(C. leuconota)* is colored somewhat like a domestic Modena pigeon. It breeds on rocks in the Himalayas above 10,000 feet, coming down to the valleys in winter. Besides a curious, hiccup-like note, it utters a "kuck, kuck, kuck" coo. It has a slaty-gray head, wings dark brownish-gray, with brown bands; its neck and under-parts are white; the tail is blackish, crossed by a V-shaped, white band. It is found from Yarkand and Kashmir to

Tibet. It thrives in confinement, where it breeds readily. Hybrids with domestic Pigeons are infertile.

The SILVER PIGEON *(C. argentina)* is a rare bird from Borneo and Sumatra, which was kept in the London Zoo in 1922. Sluggish by habit, it perches mostly on trees, somewhat like the Imperial Fruit Pigeons. Its color is very pale gray, with the quills and the tip of the tail black.

The WHITE-COLLARED PIGEON *(C. albitorques)* is bluish-slate, with irregular black bars across the wings; the feathers of the neck are long and pointed, glossed with green; it has a white nuchal collar, broadest at the back. Abyssinia is its habitat. At Cleres a specimen lived for many years and proved very hardy.

The SOMALI PIGEON *(C. oliviae),* is pale gray, with a reddish crown and hind-neck. The eye ceres are yellow.

The CONGO PIGEON *(C. unicincta),* found in West African forests, has the head, hind-neck, and upper-back gray; wings dark gray; back pale-brown; tail white, with a dark-gray tip; the breast vinous; the belly white.

The TRIANGULAR SPOTTED PIGEON *(G. guinea),* or GUINEA PIGEON, is common in captivity, where it proves hardy and breeds freely. A rather imposing bird, with the habits of the common Rock Pigeon, it lives on cliffs, rocks and buildings throughout Africa, but not in forests. It has large, very showy, red eye ceres. The neck feathers are stiff and bifid, forming a frill when the bird coos. Its voice is audible for some distance and has a distinctive, bark-like sound. This large pigeon's head, breast, rump, and quills are gray; the back and wings chestnut, with triangular white spots. Of the several subspecies, the northwestern one *(guinea)* is freely imported. The southern form *(phoenotus)* also has bred in confinement. It differs in having the gray portions of the plumage darker.

The EUROPEAN WOOD PIGEON *(C. palumbus)* is almost as familiar as the common Rock Pigeon. Even though not domesticated like the latter, it is to be found in the parks and squares of Paris, London, and other large cities, where it has become exceedingly tame, while in the country it remains wild and wary. Partly migratory, it is abundant to the point of being destructive to garden and field crops owing to its liking for green food. Its plumage is bluish-gray, with large, white patches on the

Nutmeg Imperial Pigeons (also called White Imperial Pigeon, White Fruit Pigeon) in captivity. A San Diego Zoo photo.

Opposite:
Nutmeg Imperial Pigeon *(Ducula bicolor).*

137

sides of the neck. Compared with the Rock Pigeon, it is larger, its head smaller, its wings longer, and its legs shorter. Dwelling in trees, it avoids rocks and buildings. In captivity, it needs much space. Wild-caught specimens stay wild and are inclined to injure their heads flying against the wire netting, while aviary-raised specimens may become tame. This species is found in Europe and in western Asia, with slightly different forms inhabiting the Azores, North Africa, Persia, and the Himalayas.

The MADEIRAN PIGEON *(C. trocaz)*, found also in the western Canary Islands, was at one time common, but has recently greatly decreased in number. It frequents the forests or the mountains, where it feeds on laurel berries. A very large, fine bird, its color is slaty-blue, paler on the head, lower back, rump, and under-parts; the hind-neck is glossed with green; the feathers on the sides of the neck are scale-like and tipped with silver gray; the breast is vinous-chestnut; the tail lead-gray, crossed by a broad, light gray band. The Canarian race *(bollei)* is even more attractive, its mantle being glossed with green and purple, and the sides of its neck having a coppery chestnut patch.

The CANARIAN PIGEON *(C. junoniae)*, which inhabits the islands of Palma and Gomera, is very large. Its color is gray, the head and neck green-glossed, the outer tail-feathers paler at the tips; the breast and abdomen vinous-chestnut. Occasionally it has been imported into Europe—a magnificent bird, at present rare.

A group of beautiful Wood Pigeons are found in certain parts of Asia and Africa, living in forests, often on mountains. They are a rich, dark-brown and gray, with white spots and markings. Berries and fruit constitute their principal diet.

HODGSONS'S WOOD PIGEON *(C. hodgsoni)* lives in the Himalayas and Western China at altitudes between 8,000 and 13,000 feet. It is dark vinous-purple, with gray spots and gray head and breast; its beak is gray.

The OLIVE PIGEON *(C. arquatrix)* lies in East and South Africa, the Congo and the Cameroons. A large and beautiful pigeon, it is deep purplish-chestnut, with the crown, nape, rump, and wing-edges gray. It has white spots on the back, scapulars, and lower breast; its bill, feet and eye ceres are yellow. This splendid pigeon was imported during the last thirty years and is part of the collection of Cleres, where it breeds regularly. Related species live on Sao Thome *(C. thomensis)* and the Ituri Forest of the Congo *(C. albinucha)*, the former is very large and dark, the latter smaller with a white patch on the nape.

The COMORO PIGEON *(C. polleni)*, not yet introduced, is also related to the Olive Pigeon, having yellow bill, legs and eye cere. It is brownish-gray, paler on head and rump, the feathers of nape and hind-neck long, pointed, and tipped with white.

Different Wood Pigeons, all with spotted hind-necks, live in Asia: *C. torringtoni*, Ceylon; *C. elphinstoni*, S. W. India; *C. pulchricollis*, Himalayas to Formosa, seldom kept in confinement.

The PURPLE WOOD PIGEON *(C. punicea)*, which lives in eastern Bengal and Assam, east to Indochina and south to Malaya, is mahogany-red, with purple and green reflections, bright on nape and hind-neck; the quills and tail are black; the crown in the male is white. Two pairs from Indochina lived many years at Cleres, where they proved to be a healthy and hardy species, but failed to nest.

Large and beautiful Metallic Wood Pigeons are found from the Andaman Islands and Japan to Australia. All have a dark, slate-gray plumage above, the feathers bordered with bright, metallic fringes. Many have portions of the head and under-parts, or all of them white. Only a few of these arboreal, short legged birds have found their way into captivity, where one has so far bred. This fact is the more to be regretted since these magnificent birds live long, are easily cared for, gentle, and hardy.

The JAPANESE PIGEON *(C. ianthina)* and its subspecies in the adjoining islands are blackish-slate, glossed with brilliant purple or green, according to the prevailing light.

The METALLIC PIGEON *(C. vitiensis)*, found under many races from the lesser Sunda Islands and the Philippines to New Guinea, New Caledonia, Fiji, and Samoa, is similar, with more or less gray or white on cheeks and throat, and chestnut-tinged under-parts. A few have found their way into captivity, particularly the WHITE THROATED PIGEON *(C. v. halmaheira)*, bred repeatedly in England. It lays one egg in each clutch. The FIJIAN PIGEON *(C. v. vitiensis)* also has been kept. Its forehead is gray.

A somewhat different species, with head and neck pale gray, *(C. pallidiceps)*, inhabits the Bismarck Archipelago and the Solomon

Indian Pintail Green Pigeon *(Sphenurus apicauda)*. The male has a longer tail than the female.

Opposite:
Black-naped Fruit Dove *(Ptilinopus melanospila)*. The female of this fruit dove is green and lacks the contrasting head markings seen in this photograph. A San Diego Zoo photo.

Islands, while another one, with entirely white head, neck, breast and under-parts, (*C. norfolciensis*), is found in eastern Australia.

The last group of Old World Pigeons, previously distinguished as *Turturoena,* are natives of the African forests. These smallest *Columba* have now and then been kept in British and American zoos, but there is no record of their breeding.

The GABOON BRONZE-NAPED PIGEON (*Columba iriditorques*) is fairly common in West African forests, where dwelling in tall tree tops it is difficult to catch. Its call is a very deep "coo-coo," repeated thrice on a descending scale. The male's head and upper-neck are lead gray; nape and hind-neck glossed with green, below which appears a collar of coppery feathers with amethystine reflections. The remaining upper-parts are slate-gray, the feathers of the mantle edged with green; the under-parts are vinous. The hen has a vinous head and grayish-brown under-parts.

The SAO THOME BRONZE-NAPED PIGEON (*Columba malherbei*) is slate-black, with green reflections from above and lead-gray below; the neck metallic green and purple.

DELAGORGUE'S BRONZE-NAPED PIGEON (*C. delagorguei*), from East and South Africa, is blackish above, grizzled-gray below, with crown and nape reddish-chestnut, and metallic purple reflections on the upper-back.

MAYER'S PIGEON (*C. mayeri*), from the island of Mauritius, is unlike any other species, although close to *Columba*. A moderately sized bird, it is pale buffy-pink, with back, wing, and tail brown; eyes and bill yellow; legs red. This beautiful bird is nearing extinction, which is more deplorable since the few specimens kept in captivity in the past proved quite manageable and would undoubtedly have bred under adequate conditions if so furnished. An attempt is now being made at the Jersey Zoo (Channel Islands, British Isles) to save the species by breeding it in captivity.

AMERICAN PIGEONS

Members of the genus *Columba* are numerous in the New World, especially in South America. They very much resemble those of the Old World, particularly in the Wood Pigeons. Mainly arboreal, these birds, generally, have short legs and slender bills.

The WHITE-CROWNED PIGEON *(C. leucocephala)* is dark, but handsome. This gregarious pigeon lives only on small islands in the Caribbean Sea, from Florida to Panama, its food consisting mainly of berries. Its plumage is blackish lead-gray, lighter below, with a pure white cap in the male, which is grayish in the female. The sides of the neck are glossy green, each feather edged with velvety black, forming black diagonal lines on the neck. The young lack the white on the head. This species nests readily in captivity.

The WEST INDIAN PIGEON *(C. squamosa)* is found in all Caribbean Islands excepting Jamaica. In appearance and habit it resembles the aforementioned species, but it is larger and finer: dark gray, with head, neck, and crop rich metallic violet, each feather bordered with velvety maroon. It does well in aviaries.

The PICAZURO PIGEON *(C. picazuro)*, from Brazil, Bolivia and Argentina, resembles to some extent the European Wood Pigeon, except that it is duller. Aviculturists have often kept and bred it. Its head and under-parts are vinous; the hind-neck laced with metallic greenish-gray and black; the wing sooty-brown, with white edges to the greater coverts; the mantle scaled black and purplish; the rump gray.

The NAKED-EYED PIGEON *(C. gymnophthalmos)* is similar, but has a naked, reddish-gray ring around the eyes. It is found in the dry sections of Venezuela and Colombia, and on neighboring islands. It has rosy-vinous head and neck, pale-brown wings, with a white band. It was often bred in the London Zoo.

The SPOT-WINGED PIGEON *(C. maculosa)* is another common species abundant from Peru to Patagonia, where it frequents open country. It flourishes in captivity. Its head and under-parts are gray, with a vinaceous tinge; the mantle and wing-coverts are brownish-gray, with white spots.

The FAIR PIGEON *(C. speciosa)* is a magnificently colored species, with head and wing rich-maroon, tinged purple; the feathers around neck and breast are white, laced with metallic green and purple, effecting a scaly appearance; quills, rump, and tail blackish-gray; belly white; bill and feet red. The hen is somewhat duller. This difficult-to-catch forest bird has never been common in captivity. Although this very beautiful pigeon will breed in aviaries, it usually remains rather shy and clumsy.

Thick-billed Green Pigeon *(Treron curvirostra)* (male).

Although Thick-billed Green Pigeons eat mostly fruit and berries, it has been observed that figs attract them the most. Photo by A.J. Mobbs.

Large Green Pigeon *(Treron capellei),* male (above), female (below).

The group of the Rufous Pigeons, all fairly alike, include five species:

The RED-BILLED PIGEON *(C. flavirostris)*, from the high forests of Mexico and Central America, often feeding on acorns, breeds mainly in the North, and lays but one egg. Its head, neck, upper-back and breast are vinous-red; the chin and throat whitish; wing-coverts reddish-vinous; mantle, back, wings and tail gray, with quills and greater coverts edged white; the belly is gray; the bill rosy-red, tipped with white; a red eye cere encircles the eyes. It has been fairly often imported, and there are several subspecies.

The PLAIN PIGEON *(C. inornata)*, with three subspecies, lives in the Greater Antilles. It is very similar, but larger. Its mantle is brownish-gray, the back and rump are bluish; head, neck, upper-back, and under-parts reddish-vinous; the bill is black. It has been imported several times.

The PERUVIAN PIGEON *(C. oenops)* resembles *flavirostris*, but its mantle and wing coverts are vinaceous-red; its crown grayish purple; its bill red.

The JAMAICAN PIGEON *(C. caribaea)* has a black bill; it is gray above; the tail is crossed in the center by a black band; the hind-neck is metallic green, shot with purple; head, neck, and under-parts vinous. As its name suggests, it hails from Jamaica.

This group extends to South America with the smaller RUFOUS PIGEON *(G. rufina)*. It is darker and more richly colored, and it has a black bill. Its nape has green reflections; its mantle and upper-back are shot with purple; the throat is white; the face gray; the crown, mantle and breast are vinous; belly pale gray; back and rump bluish. It has proved a free breeder in confinement. Its various races are found from southern Mexico, Colombia, Ecuador, the Guianas, Trinidad, and Tobago, south to Brazil and Paraguay.

The Band-tailed Pigeons constitute another important group of American species characterized by a gray and vinous plumage, a black band in the center of the tail, a narrow, white nuchal band with a patch of metallic green on the hind-neck below. They are found from British Columbia through the West Coast of North America, Colombia, Venezuela, and south along the Andes to the forested mountains of Argentina and Chile, always in temperate regions. So similar are the three species that at present it has been recognized that they should probably be united.

The BAND-TAILED PIGEON *(C. fasciata)* is the only species of Wood Pigeon living in Canada and the United States, where it is restricted to the West Coast. Its behavior is like that of the European Wood Pigeon. It is just beginning to frequent gardens in southern California, thus imitating its European counterpart. It thrives in captivity in large enough pens, proving hardy and feeding on grain. To keep it, a special state permit is required. It is a handsome bird; head, fore-neck, and under-parts purplish-gray, fading to white under the tail; back, wings, and tail brownish-gray, the last-mentioned having a black band in the center; a white line appears on the nape, followed by a golden-green patch; the bill is yellow and tipped black; the legs are yellow. Other subspecies live in Mexico and Central America.

The WHITE-NAPED PIGEON *(C. albilinea)* is very similar, only darker, with crown and under-parts deep grayish vinous and a wholly yellow beak. This pigeon ranges from Costa Rica, where the local race *(crissalis)* is paler and grayer below, to southeastern Venezuela, and along the Andes to Tucuman. Occasionally it has been imported.

The CHILEAN PIGEON *(C. araucana)* is even darker and more richly colored, with head, upper-back, and under-parts dark chestnut-vinous, and upper-parts blackish-brown, tinged green. The bill is black; the feet are pink-red. Epidemics have greatly reduced the once large numbers of this Chilean pigeon, which has proved itself hardy and easy to care for in captivity, where it has been bred in European aviaries.

Five rather small species complete the group of South American *Columba*—all uniformly vinous on head and under-parts, and brown above, with black bills. None seems to have been imported. Moreover, they are not ornamental: *C. goodsoni* from the lowlands of western Colombia and Ecuador; *C. nigrirostris* from southern Mexico and Central America; *C. subvinacea* from Costa Rica to Venezuela and Bolivia; *C. plumbea* from Colombia, Ecuador, Peru, Bolivia, and Brazil; *C. chiriquensis* from Panama.

GYMNOPHAPS

A fine genus of large pigeons akin to *Columba* live in the Moluccas, New Guinea, and nearby islands, providing a link with the

Orange-breasted Green Pigeon *(Treron bicincta)*; the male is the lower bird.

Pompadour Green Pigeon *(Treron pompadora),* pair; the male is the lower bird.

Fruit Pigeons and being classified as *Gymnophaps*. The three species are: *G. albertisi* (two subspecies), which is dark gray above, with face, throat, and belly chestnut, and breast white; bill, feet, and eye cere yellow. Next comes *G. solomonensis*, pale gray, darker on wings and mantle, with a pinkish-white belly; and, finally, *G. mada* (two subspecies), which is dark gray above, pale on the crown; face, throat, and under-parts pink cinnamon; eye cere yellow. To my knowledge, none of these beautiful pigeons has yet been kept in confinement.

Large Ground Pigeons

Here we group four genera of very large pigeons from New Guinea and the smaller islands in the Indian and Pacific Oceans. Though they are not closely related, it is convenient to place them here.

The NICOBAR PIGEON *(Caloenas nicobarica)*, a remarkable bird, is the size of a large bantam chicken. It has long, narrow neck hackles, but very short head feathers. It has a strong, hooked bill and large feet with long claws. Its general color is metallic green, with coppery reflections; the head and flight feathers are slate-black; the very short tail and its under-coverts are pure white. Nicobar Pigeons have a very small, black knob at the base of the bill, near the forehead; it is larger in the male. The female is smaller and more copper-colored, with shorter neck hackles. The young are without hackles; their tails are slaty-gray, glossed green. Nicobar Pigeons are quite insular in habits, roosting and breeding only on small, uninhabited islets, whence they fly to larger islands in the daytime to feed. They are found throughout the largest part of the Indo-Australian region, from the Nicobars to the Philippines, New Guinea, and the Solomons. A very slightly different subspecies, smaller and bluer, inhabits the Palaus. These splendid pigeons seek their food on the ground, where they toss leaves aside and dig with their bills. In safe localities, they live in large numbers, but if their haunts are invaded, they are much exposed to attacks by man and mammals. They live and breed well in captivity. The youngster that hatches from the single egg stays in the nest for nearly three months. These large, lovely pigeons feed on various seeds and grains, being fond of corn. While they are reasonably hardy, it is best to protect them against severe frost. Since they are large and powerful flyers, they need roomy accommodations. Baskets or boxes hung high serve them well as nests.

Cinnamon-headed Green Pigeon *(Treron fulvicollis)*. The male (lower bird) is strikingly different in coloration.

Burmese Yellow-legged Green Pigeon *(Treron phoenicoptera viridifrons)*. The race from Burma and Thailand has bright greenish yellow forehead.

Altogether, Nicobar Pigeons, owing to their unique appearance and large size, are very popular with dove keepers. Moreover, they are peaceful and do not harm other birds.

The PHEASANT PIGEONS *(Otidiphaps nobilis)* are magnificent. Though almost as large as the Nicobar, their legs and tails are much longer. New Guinea and neighboring islands are their home. Since they are very game-bird-like, they resemble a small pheasant in shape. In confinement they are exceedingly rare, although the four races have been in the collections of the London Zoo, Cleres, Foxwarren, and a few others in Europe during the last thirty years. Between 1930 and 1937, many were reared by Mrs. Black near Los Angeles, Calif. Not only are they shy, but they usually remain wild. A warm aviary, well planted with thick shrubbery and other more or less natural hiding places is to their liking. Their walk is jerky, bobbing their tails up and down. At night they roost high. Their nests are found at the foot of bushes or trees, containing one egg each. In addition to grain and berries, they should be given some animal food.

The subspecies found on the mountains of western New Guinea, *nobilis,* has an occipital crest. Its general color is greenish-black, bluer on the rump, lower neck, and sides of the neck; the hind-neck is bronze-green; the mantle golden; the back and wings purplish-chestnut; the bill and legs are a bright vermilion. The sexes are alike. The Aru Islands subspecies, *aruensis,* is very similar.

The eastern New Guinea form, *cervicalis,* has a shorter crest, which is hardly noticeable. It has a gray instead of a green nape, and its back is greener.

The subspecies from Ferguson Island, *insularis,* is smaller, blacker, duller and without the nape patch. Unfortunately, since they live on the forest floor in remote, high country, they are difficult to catch. Their "mourning" coo is audible for a considerable distance; and when imitated, they answer it readily, stalking to and fro with tail erect and spread, as if to challenge the intruder. When disturbed, they fly into low trees, though generally they escape by walking away.

The mysterious Pigmy Goura *(Microgoura meeki)* found only once on Choiseul Island, Solomons, is probably extinct. Like the Goura, it has a crest, but is much smaller.

Close-up of the head of a Victoria Crowned Pigeon *(Goura victoria)*. Blue is the predominant color of Crowned Pigeons. A Muller-Schmida photo.

The Crowned Pigeons *(Goura)*, by far the largest and perhaps the most magnificent of all pigeons, approach turkeys in size. Huge, fanlike crests, composed of feathers with separated barbs, lend a unique and striking adornment. Their tails are long; their legs, strong, high, and red; their eyes bright ruby; their general color slaty blue-gray, with maroon-chestnut patches. All three species are found in and about New Guinea. Crowned Pigeons have long been great favorites with zoos and private collectors, few birds excelling them in beauty. As long as they are well sheltered during the winter, they are easy to keep. But they cannot stand frost, which soon injures their tender, fleshy feet. Naturally, they require ample space. Their food consists of grain and some animal food. Although they are usually harmless to smaller birds, they

155

Yellow-legged Green Pigeon *(Treron phoenicoptera)*. Males and females resemble each other, although the plumage of the female is duller. A San Diego Zoo photo.

Opposite:
Yellow-bellied Green Pigeon
(Treron waalia). A San Diego Zoo
photo.

can be dangerous to larger ones, which they strike with their powerful wings. They breed readily, taking several months to rear their young. Large boxes or baskets should be hung for their nests.

The BLUE-CROWNED PIGEON *(Goura cristata)* inhabits northwest New Guinea, with a slightly smaller race, *minor*, on the islands of Misol, Salawatti, Batana and Waigeu. It is a superb bird, two and one-half feet long, bluish-gray, darker on wings and tail, the latter with a broad, pale gray band at the tip; a black band runs through the eyes; a wide band across the back and the tips of the upper wing coverts are maroon-chestnut; the medium wing-coverts are barred with white. The crest consists of feathers decomposed to the tip. These *Goura* live mostly on the forest floors searching for seeds and berries, as well as for grubs and insects. Since they are very tame, they can be approached easily. Their nest, set in trees, contains a single, large, white egg. This species has been kept longer and oftener in captivity than the others. When it is warm enough, it can be let out into gardens, where it stays well.

SCLATER'S CROWNED PIGEON *(Goura scheepmakeri)*, which occurs in southeastern and southern New Guinea, is less often imported than the other two species. It differs from *cristata* in having a blue-gray instead of chestnut back; its fore-neck and breast are maroon-chestnut. The Southeastern form differs from the Southern *(sclateri)* in having grayish-blue in place of chestnut lesser wing-coverts, pale gray instead of pure white wing-patches, and paler gray tips of the crest feathers. Sclater's Crowned Pigeons are common in their native forests, where early in the morning, in groups of two or three, they forage along muddy river-banks. Remnants of small crabs have been found in their stomachs. When disturbed, they turn around with raised wings and crest before taking flight, a common habit with all *Goura*. They take shelter in high trees after ponderous, strong, straight flight. Both races have been in zoological and private collections, but there is no evidence of their breeding in captivity.

The VICTORIA CROWNED PIGEON *(Goura victoria)* differs from the other species in that its crest feathers are spatulated at the tip, each spatula being white-edged. Perhaps it is the handsomest of all. The typical race is found on the islands of Jobi and Biak, while another one *(beccarii)*—larger and stronger, with wider

The white tips of the crest feathers distinguish the Victoria Crowned Pigeon from other members of the genus *Goura.* A New York Zoological Society photo.

Black-naped Fruit Dove
(Ptilinopus melanospila),
male. Photo courtesy of
Vogelpark Walsrode).

Orange-fronted Fruit Dove
(Ptilinopus aurantiifrons).
Photo courtesy of Vogelpark
Walsrode.

crest spatulas—inhabits northern New Guinea. Both have been imported, and it is difficult to tell them apart. In color pattern they are like Sclaters's Crowned Pigeon, having also the fore-neck and breast maroon-chestnut, but darker and richer, and bluish-gray wing-bars. This lovely bird has often been reared in captivity in Europe, America, and elsewhere; it acts exactly like the other two Crowned Pigeons. For large, warm enclosures it is one of the most attractive and desirable occupants.

At this point, we mention the most curious of all pigeons, characterized by its thick, hooked bill, the lower mandible serrated near the truncated tip, recalling that of the huge, long-extinct Dodos of Mauritius and Reunion.

The TOOTH-BILLED PIGEON *(Didunculus strigirostris)*, from Samoa (Upolu and Savaii), formerly a ground bird, changed its habits after near-extermination by introduced cats, rats, and other pests. Now it roosts and nests in trees. It is very shy. Its food consists of fruit and berries. Its flight is powerful and noisy. The size of a large dove, its head, neck, mantle, and upper-breast are metallic dark green; the lower breast and belly brownish-black; the rest of the upper-parts chestnut. The bill is orange, the eye ceres are red. The sexes are alike. Only a few specimens have ever found their way to Europe, where they have always been regarded as precious rarities. They have laid in captivity.

Fruit Pigeons

The Fruit Pigeons *(Treroninae)* constitutes a well-defined and special group of *Columbidae*, as opposed to the seed-eating species so far considered. Their legs *(tarsi)* are extremely short; the soles of their feet are large, the toes being widened and flattened on the sides by a skin extension. Most of them have a bright, mainly green, plumage, often enlivened with yellow, red, pink and other gay colors rivalling parrots in their gaudy attire. All live on trees, in forests or savannas, where they feed on soft fruits and berries. Even though their bills are usually weak and soft, the wide gape enables them to swallow large fruits with pits. Their stomach, which is adapted to such a diet, differs from that of other pigeons in this respect. Banyan figs and nutmegs are their usual staple food.

Most Fruit Pigeons are sedentary, wandering only in search of trees bearing ripe fruit, but a few migrate. Many live in flocks most of the time. Their strong, fast flights often produce a whistling noise, but they themselves are stolid, remaining quiet for a long time. In their ways they are abrupt and not very shy, returning again and again to a favorite perch. However, they often remain motionless and are not easy to locate in the foliage. Many species have a harsh, raucous call, but a few utter a pleasing, flute-like coo. They nest when fruit is abundant, building in the trees the usual casual platform of the family, and laying only one egg in each clutch.

Despite their strikingly beautiful plumage, Fruit Pigeons are rarely seen in captivity. Most aviculturists shun them because of their special food requirements, the mess their soft food causes, and their sluggish behavior. It is difficult to transport them in good condition as they get easily soiled, unless they are kept very clean in cages with false bottoms of wire netting. Nevertheless,

Although Fruit Pigeons in captivity will survive on other types of food, fruit should be made part of their diet. The author is shown nailing fruit on the wall of the aviary. Photo by L. van der Meid.

these draw-backs can be fairly easily overcome. Fruit Pigeons make really splendid aviary birds if they can be given sufficient space, for then they remain very clean. On arrival, they must be kept warm, but once acclimatized many prove hardy. Since they require much fresh air, they should be kept outdoors as much as possible. The food most suitable for them is boiled rice and corn (maize), chopped-up dried figs, raisins, diced boiled potatoes, soaked dog-biscuit, pellets and chicken mash, to which some cut-up, fresh fruit such as bananas, apples, and grapes are added in fairly small amounts. Most Fruit Pigeons will readily take to boiled corn, pellets, biscuit, and mash as a staple diet. Many will eat even some dry grain, although they do not digest it well. To prevent the soiling of their feathers, particularly around the bill, their food should be cut up to small grape size, the soft fruits powdered with bread crumbs or corn meal, and offered in clean, small vessels. Planted aviaries suit Fruit Pigeons best; they will nest in baskets and boxes fastened to walls and trees. They need numerous perches as they seldom come to the ground, on which they walk, or, rather, hop, with some difficulty; but they climb deftly among branches. To other birds they are usually harmless, although pairs of the same species will fight savagely and should be separated.

Only few Fruit Pigeons have bred in confinement, which is due to lack of adequate care and accommodation, as many actually nest readily. When you consider the numerous existing species, it is astonishing that so many beautiful ones have been imported rarely, if indeed at all. The unwarranted assumption that their maintenance is difficult has relegated them largely to public zoos; fanciers have been reluctant to try them in their aviaries—in my opinion, wrongly so.

Owing to this lack of popularity, I will review the numerous species of Fruit Pigeons only briefly. But I hope thus to call the reader's attention to these gorgeously colored birds, which deserve a prominent place in aviculture.

Fruit Pigeons are found in the Old World in Africa, southern and eastern Asia, Malaysia, Australia, and the numerous Pacific Islands, special, lovely species being restricted to some of the smaller ones. The three principal groups of Fruit Pigeons are: the large Imperial Fruit Pigeons of the genus *Ducula* and allies, which recall in appearance and size the pigeons of the genus *Columba*, and are found in southern Asia, Malaysia, Australia, and the Pacific Islands; the Green Pigeons (*Treron* and allies), of Africa, southern and eastern Asia, the Philippines, Celebes, and Malaysia; and the Fruit Doves (*Ptilonopus* and others) of the Philippines, Malaysia, Australia, and the Pacific Islands.

IMPERIAL FRUIT PIGEONS

This group is composed of large, heavily-built pigeons with big heads, thick necks, weak bills, flat nostrils, and thick, purplish-red legs and feet. The sexes, with one exception, are alike. They practically never descend to the ground, feeding on fruit in trees.

Their flexible mandibles and wide gape enable them to swallow many large berries with huge pits, which later they reject. Their voice is a low, harsh, and booming coo. Superficially they look like large Wood Pigeons, only heavier in shape. Green appears in the plumage of many species. They adapt themselves to captive conditions, provided they are afforded much room. They feed readily on chicken mash, pellets, soaked biscuit, boiled corn and potato, even on uncooked grain.

A first group of Pacific species is characterized by a fleshy protuberance at the base of the bill, on the forehead.

The PACIFIC IMPERIAL PIGEON *(Ducula pacifica)* is found under four local forms in the islands west of New Guinea, including the New Hebrides, Tonga, Fiji, and Samoa. Its head, neck, and upper-back are gray; its upper-parts dark green; its throat and under-parts vinous; the bill is black. It is occasionally imported.

The OCEANIC FRUIT PIGEON *(D. oceanica)*, which lives in the Caroline and Marshall Islands, is similar, but has a dark gray head and hind-neck, a light gray breast, and a chestnut belly.

The Tahiti *(D. aurorae)* and Nuka-Hiva *(D. galeata)* species belong to the same group, as does also the Bismarck Archipelago and Solomon species *(D. rubricera)*. All are very large, with a big knob, dark green above; head, neck and lower-parts pinky-white, changing to cinnamon on the belly. The Solomon species has the crown gray, the upper-back and breast cinnamon; it has been imported.

The other species of *Ducula* lack the knob on the forehead:

The NEW GUINEA IMPERIAL PIGEON *(D. myristicivora)* has gray head, upper-back, and breast, vinous under-parts, and dark green upper-parts.

The BLUE-TAILED IMPERIAL PIGEON *(D. concinna)* is similar, except that underneath it is gray. This pigeon, which comes from Celebes and the Moluccas, is fairly often seen in aviaries.

The GREEN IMPERIAL PIGEON *(D. aenea)* is the best-known and most often kept in confinement. With numerous subspecies, it is found from India to Indochina, the Philippines to Malaysia and Celebes. It is light, grayish-green above, pale gray below; the western races have the face, nape and belly tinged

A Green Imperial Pigeon *(Ducula aenea)* usually builds its nest on young trees which are not too high. Only one egg is laid.

vinaceous-red. It has nested successfully in Mr. M.M. Strann's aviaries near Los Angeles on several occasions.

D. pistrinaria, from the Solomons and nearby islands, is dark green above and pinkish on the throat.

The CHRISTMAS ISLAND IMPERIAL PIGEON *(D. whartoni)* is oddly colored: blackish, with green and purple reflections. The London Zoo has kept it.

The PINK IMPERIAL PIGEON *(D. rosacea),* from the Lesser Sunda Islands, resembles *aenea,* but it is pink-vinous on the underparts and has reddish-buff feathers on the head.

The SPECTACLED IMPERIAL PIGEON *(D. perspicillata),* from the Moluccas, has a dark gray head and neck, with a pale eye cere. Its upper-parts are deep metallic green; its under-parts light-gray. It has been imported.

The GRAY IMPERIAL PIGEON *(D. pickeringi)* is comparatively small and dull, gray below, brownish-gray above. Its home is the small islands between Borneo, the Philippines and Celebes.

The FIJI IMPERIAL PIGEON *(D. latrans)* is dark brown above, vinous below, with sides of head and upper-back gray. It has been imported.

D. bakeri from the New Hebrides, and *D. brenchleyi,* from the Solomons, also are dark-brown above, with head and upper-back gray, under-parts deep-chestnut; the latter is darker.

The GOLIATH IMPERIAL PIGEON *(D. goliath),* from New Caledonia, the giant of the genus, has the head, upper-back and breast dark gray, the feathers pointed; upper-parts blackish-brown; belly and lesser wing-coverts chestnut.

The White Nutmeg Pigeons constitute a special group; they live on islets from the Andamans to Australia. Their white plumage is tinged with yellow and their wings and tails are gray or black-tipped.

The NUTMEG IMPERIAL PIGEON *(D. bicolor)* is milky-white with black primaries, secondaries and tail tip. It has often been kept in aviaries. It inhabits numerous small islands between India, the Philippines, and New Guinea.

The closely allied *D. luctuosa,* from Celebes, has gray wings and tail; *D. melanura,* from the Moluccas, is like *bicolor,* but has black spots on the vent and thighs; *D. spilorrhoa,* from New Guinea and Australia, is spotted even more. All live well in aviaries.

The following species are mainly gray or brown above, gray and vinous below:

D. cineracea, from Timor and Wetar; gray head and upper-back; dark gray upper parts; and vinous under-parts.

D. lacernulata, from the mountains of Java, Bali, Lombok, and Flores, is slate-gray above, vinous-gray below, while its black tail is tipped with gray to mark it somewhat.

The MOUNTAIN IMPERIAL PIGEON *(D. badia)* found in the highlands of India, Indochina, Yunnan, and Malaysia, with several races, has the head, neck and upper-parts dark brown; the under-parts pale vinaceous-gray; throat and cheeks white; vent and under tail-coverts cinnamon; tail black, tipped gray. The bill is partly red.

MULLER'S IMPERIAL PIGEON *(D. mulleri),* from New Guinea, has been imported. Its crown is fulvous-brown; its chin, throat and an occipital collar are white; a lower collar is black; the

White and black are the dominant colors in the Nutmeg Imperial Pigeon *(Ducula bicolor)*. The white parts, especially near the neck and head, are stained by fruit juices. A New York Zoological Society photo.

Opposite:
In this position the collars (an
upper white and a lower black) of a
Muller's Imperial Pigeon are clearly seen.
A New York Zoological Society photo.

fore-neck and upper-breast are gray; the back is vinous-red; the mantle slate gray; the tail is dark gray, tipped with pale gray.

The PINON IMPERIAL PIGEON *(D. pinon)*, likewise from New Guinea and neighboring islands, has a vinaceous-gray head and neck, with white lines around the bill and eyes; the upper-back is slate-gray; upper-parts and breast purplish-chestnut. It has been imported several times.

D. melanochlora, from the Bismarck Archipelago, is dark slate gray with the wings laced pale gray, a dark chestnut vent and under tail-coverts.

Two magnificent species inhabit the Philippines and Celebes:

The MINDORO IMPERIAL PIGEON *(D. mindorensis),* one of the largest and finest, has the face, throat, and fore-crown pinkish-buff; a black line behind the eye; remainder of head and under-parts pale gray; upper-parts bright copper-green, the mantle black; the tail is blue-black; with a broad, gray band across the center. This pigeon is very rare and confined to the island of Mindoro.

The GRAY-FACED PIGEON *(D. poliocephala),* from the Philippines and Celebes, has the head pale gray, washed with green on occiput and nape; the chin and upper throat are cinnamon; neck, breast, upper-parts, and tail emerald-green, the tail with a broad, gray band in the center, the under-parts are vinaceous-pink in the Philippine birds, white in the Celebes *(forsteni);* the vent and under tail-coverts are chestnut.

D. radiata (Celebes) is small and gray, with chestnut on the mantle and under the tail, green wings and tail.

The RED-BREASTED IMPERIAL PIGEON *(D. rufigaster)* from the Moluccas, New Guinea and adjoining island coasts; varies with the localities. Its head and breast are pinkish; its upper-back gray; mantle chestnut; wings dark-green; tail black or chestnut, tipped gray; and under-parts cinnamon.

FINSCH'S IMPERIAL PIGEON *(D. finschi),* from the Bismarck Archipelago, has the head and neck vinaceous-gray, breast and belly pinkish red-cinnamon; mantle copper-red; wings bluish-green; tail blue, near the tip ashy-gray and black.

D. chalconota, from New Guinea's mountains, has a dark gray crown and upper-back, cinnamon throat and under-parts, dark-green upper-parts, and a black, gray-tipped tail.

ZOE'S IMPERIAL PIGEON *(D. zoeae),* also from New Guinea, has a gray head; a vinous upper-back; a black band on the breast; chestnut mantle and wings; green back and tail; and chestnut under-parts. It has been imported.

The SPOTTED IMPERIAL PIGEON *(D. carola),* from the Philippine mountains, is rather small, and since male and female differ, exceptional. The male has a gray head and upper-back, a whitish throat, gray back and wings, spotted with black, metallic green rump and flight feathers, a blue tail, a gray upper-breast, and a darker belly. The hen has a green mantle. There are several well-marked subspecies.

A somewhat unique Fruit Pigeon is *Cryptophaps poecilorrhoa,* from the mountains of Celebes, rare and peculiar. It has a long tail and small bill, it is gray with dark brown upper parts.

The large Fruit Pigeons of New Zealand and neighboring islands also have a special shape: long tail and wings and relatively small head and bill.

The NEW ZEALAND PIGEON *(Hemiphaga novaeseelandiae)* has the head, neck, upper-breast and upper-back golden-green, with a coppery-purple tinge on the mantle, and white under-parts. Two closely related races inhabit the Norfolk and Chatham islands. This beautiful species, now scarce, seems not to have ever been imported.

The TOP-KNOT PIGEON *(Lopholaimus antarcticus)* of Australia, colored like a *Columba,* is gray and rusty-brown, with a double crest, the frontal one gray, the occipital rusty-red; there are black lines on the face. Although of good size and striking shape, and very hardy, this pigeon has seldom found its way into confinement. Since it keeps to the tall tree tops, it is very difficult to catch.

FRUIT DOVES

This group of Fruit Doves, the most beautiful of all pigeons, is widely distributed throughout the South Pacific Islands, reaching Malaysia and the Philippines toward Asia, and Australia, but not New Zealand, in the South. In New Guinea and throughout the smaller islands they are especially well represented. An almost incredible variety of bright colors marks their plumage. In size they vary considerably, some being very small, hardly bigger than a sparrow, while a few are almost as large as domestic pigeons. Their bills are small, their legs very short; being wholly arboreal, they naturally feed on fruit and berries. They lay only one egg in each clutch. Sometimes the females differ from the males in color, some being more-or-less uniform green.

Many of these colorful doves have lived in captivity, but only a few have bred. Nevertheless, they certainly deserve to be kept more extensively, as they flourish in aviaries which can be heated during cold weather. Moreover, they are as decorative as the gaudiest parrakeets.

The CLOVEN-FEATHERED FRUIT DOVE *(Drepanoptila holosericea)* is short-tailed and fairly large—the size of a Turtle Dove. The center of its throat is white; a black bar separates the green breast from the olive-yellow belly; the vent and under tail-coverts are yellow; the remainder of the plumage is bright green with a few pale gray bars on the wings and tail. The hen is smaller and greener below. The wing primaries are divided at the tip, a unique feature. This handsome dove is indigenous to New Caledonia.

A very large number of species are usually placed in the genus *Ptilinopus*. A first group of the species, which can be assembled in the subgenera *Megaloprepia* and *Leucotreron*, are quite large, long-tailed, and largely light-colored, especially white, yellow, pink and green.

The MAGNIFICENT FRUIT DOVE *(P. magnificus)*, a gorgeous, large, long-tailed species, is found in eastern Australia, New Guinea, and neighboring islands, the Australian races being the largest. Their coloring is as follows: the head is gray; upper-parts bright green, with yellow patches on the wings; the neck is green with a rich purplish-crimson band in front which broadens on the breast and belly. The sexes are alike. This splendid dove has been kept in captivity, particularly in the greenhouses at Cleres, but has failed to nest.

A smaller species, *P. formosus,* inhabits the Moluccas.

The YELLOW-BREASTED FRUIT DOVE *(P. occipitalis)* of the Philippines is now in American collections. Its crown, sides of neck and breast are pale-gray; its throat, face and forehead are washed with yellow; the cheeks and nape purplish-crimson: the upper-parts green; the center of the breast ochraceous-yellow, followed by a broad belt of crimson and one of lavender gray; the belly is bluish green and white. Both male and female are alike in color.

FISCHER'S FRUIT DOVE *(P. fischeri)*, from Celebes, is green and blackish-green above, greenish below, with a gray head and a red face.

MARCHE'S FRUIT DOVE *(P. marchei)* is very large and perhaps the most colorful of the species in this group. The male's crown and face are deep red; his ear-coverts black; his throat cinnamon; his upper-parts bluish-black; his primaries bordered with yellow; the secondaries broadly fringed with crimson; his tail is green; his neck and breast pale gray, the center brilliant vermilion-red, passing to dark scarlet; the lower breast is yellowish white and the belly gray. The hen, smaller and darker, is green above, mottled green and yellow below. Indigenous to the mountains of Luzon and Polillo of the Philippines, this dove is very rare.

MERRILL'S FRUIT DOVE *(P. merrilli)*, slightly smaller, is found on the same islands and is even rarer. It is green above with the head and neck paler, changing to gray on throat and upper breast, the gray being separated from the pale yellow of the lower breast and belly by a dark green line; the secondaries show a small, crimson fringe, and the primaries a white border. A northern Luzon subspecies has a red patch on the crown.

The CHESTNUT-CHINNED FRUIT DOVE *(P. subgularis)*, from Celebes, Peling and Banggai, has head and under parts gray; upper parts green, with chestnut purple chin and middle of throat; chestnut vent and under tail-coverts. The hen is green.

The BLACK-CHINNED FRUIT DOVE *(P. leclancheri)* is similar, except for a black chin and a purplish maroon breast patch. This dove, from the Philippines, is sometimes imported into the United States.

The BLACK-BACKED FRUIT DOVE *(P. cinctus)* has the head, neck, upper breast and upper back white or pale gray; the upper parts greenish black; the tail tipped gray; the lower breast black; the belly olive yellow; the vent and under tail-coverts bright yellow. It is found from Bali through the Lesser Sunda Islands, to Northern Australia, represented by numerous races.

DOHERTY'S FRUIT DOVE *(P. dohertyi)* from Sumba, has a white head, pink breast and upper back, crimson nape, dark red tail, the remaining plumage being black, and grayish on the belly. It is a rare and beautiful species.

The PINK-NECKED FRUIT DOVE *(P. porphyreus)*, indigenous to Sumatra, Java, and Bali, has on occasion been kept. It's head, neck, and upper back are crimson pink; the upper-parts are green, with blue patches on the wings; the tail tipped gray; there is a double band on the lower breast of white and greenish-black; the belly is gray and olive yellow. The sexes are the same. This dove thrives in captivity.

The JAMBU FRUIT DOVE *(P. jambu)* inhabits Malaya, Sumatra, and Borneo; it is sometimes imported. The male's chin and upper-throat are blackish-maroon; his crown, sides of head, and a border to the throat vivid crimson-pink; his upper parts green; his under parts ivory-white with a light pink patch on the breast; his under tail-coverts are chestnut. The female is green, with the forehead and chin brownish-crimson; her lower belly is white.

The following species are smaller and their plumage is dominantly green:

The BLACK-NAPED FRUIT DOVE *(P. melanospila)* is represented by many races throughout Java, the Philippines, Celebes, the Moluccas, and on many small islands. The male is emerald green, with the head and neck very pale gray; golden yellow chin and throat; black occiput and nape; lower belly and vent yellow; the under tail-coverts carmine red. The female is green. This species has often been kept in Europe.

The MANY-COLORED FRUIT DOVE *(P. perousei)*, from Samoa, Fiji, and Tonga, has its crown and a bar across the upper-back lavender-red; nape, sides of head, and under-parts yellowish-white; a pink spot in the center of the breast; upper-parts green; back and rump yellowish; wing-coverts and tail gray with greenish-yellow edges. The female is green above, grayish below, with a crimson crown and under tail-coverts. This dove has been imported.

P. coralensis, from the Tuamotu and Society Islands, is grayish and yellowish-green, and has a violet crown. *P. insularis*, from Henderson Island, and *P. huttoni*, from Rapa Island, are quite similar.

P. mercieri, from the Marquesas, has rosy-crimson crown and cheeks, yellow under-parts, and green upper-parts.

P. dupetithouarsi, also from the Marquesas, has a white cap; gray neck and breast; orange belly; gray sides and vent; grayish-green upper-parts, the wing with yellow borders; the tail green, tipped with gray.

P. purpuratus, from Tahiti and Moorea, is fairly similar, gray, with green upper-parts; its crown is lilac.

P. roratongensis is likewise similar, except for a crimson cap and patch on the belly.

The CRIMSON-CROWNED FRUIT DOVE *(P. porphyraceus)*, from the Fiji, Tonga, Samoa, Uvea, Palau, the Caroline and Marshall Islands, has a crimson cap and belly patch, varying in tone with the subspecies, yellowish-gray under-parts and green upper-parts; yellow borders on wing and tip of tail; yellow or red vent, and crimson under tail coverts. The London Zoo has kept this species.

P. greyi, from New Caledonia and the New Hebrides, has the crown purplish pink, margined with yellow; the chin and throat yellow; the remainder of head, neck, and breast greenish-gray; the upper-parts are dark green; on the belly is a dull purple patch; the vent is purple tinged with orange; the wings have gray spots and yellow margins.

P. richardsi, from the eastern Solomons, has the head and breast gray; throat yellow; upper-parts green with wings and tip of tail yellow-margined; pink spots on the scapulars; orange belly and under tail-coverts.

The PINK-CROWNED FRUIT DOVE *(P. roseicapilia)*, from the Marianas, has been kept in Japan. Its coloration includes a crimson crown; green head, breast and upper-parts; a dark crimson bar on the lower breast; and an orange belly.

SWAINSON'S FRUIT DOVE *(P. regina)*, found from the eastern Lesser Sunda Islands to northern and eastern Australia, is green with a lilac-pink crown (gray on some races), surrounded by a yellow line; yellow borders to the scapulars; pale yellow chin; throat and upper-breast are green; the lower breast and belly have beautiful patches of orange, lilac, and yellow; the under tail is orange. The female is greener.

The LILAC-CROWNED FRUIT DOVE *(P. coronulatus)*, from New Guinea and the neighboring islands, is green with a lilac crown, bordered with yellow, and a small violet patch on the belly; vent and under tail-coverts yellow; some races have an orange abdomen. This small and pretty Fruit Dove has bred repeatedly in England in Capt. S. Stokes' outdoor aviary with attached heated shelter. One egg was laid in a basket and hatched after eighteen days.

P. monachus, from the Moluccas, is also green, with a lead-blue cap, a white chin, and a yellow vent.

The PRETTY FRUIT DOVE *(P. pulchellus)*, one of the smallest and handsomest species, comes from New Guinea. Several specimens lived for many years in the tropical aviaries at Cleres, but they never laid. This attractive dove has a crimson crown, a white throat, a pale gray breast, with a crimson band and an orange belly; its upper-parts are green.

The SUPERB FRUIT DOVE *(P. superbus)*, which has several races, extends from the Sulu Archipelago and Celebes to Australia. The male's crown is purplish-red; the nape, hind-neck and sides of the breast are ochraceous-orange; behind the eye is a green patch; the chin is white; throat and breast are pearl-gray, changing to a mottled mauve; the lower breast has a black bar; the belly is yellow with green patches; the flanks, thighs, and upper-parts are green; the wing is spotted with black. The hen is green and has a yellowish-white patch on the belly; a gray chin and throat; a duller red crown and a bluish wash on the breast. This colorful little Fruit Dove has found its way to aviaries several times.

RIVOLI'S FRUIT DOVE *(P. rivoli)*, from the islands west of New Guinea, is green, with a violet cap; a broad; white band on the breast, which has a violet patch; and a yellow belly.

P. miquelli, from the islands of Gelvink Bay, is closely related.

The PURPLE-BELLIED FRUIT DOVE *(P. bellus)* is likewise similar, but green underneath, with a light yellow crescent on the breast. It is a native of New Guinea and it has been imported.

The SOLOMON FRUIT DOVE *(P. solomonensis)* is found in the Bismarck and Solomon Islands, with numerous local races. It is green, very richly colored on the head and neck, with a violet cap, a yellow breast-patch bordered with gray, a violet belly, yellow vent and under tail-coverts.

P. viridis, from the Moluccas, has gray crown and chin, crimson throat and breast, green upper-parts, with gray spots on the wing.

P. eugeniae, from the Solomon and D'Entrecasteau Islands, is similar, with a white head.

P. pectoralis has a crimson patch on the breast.

P. hyogastra, from Halmahera and Batjan, is green with gray spots on the wings; gray head; purple-red patch on the belly; the vent and under tail-coverts are yellow.

P. granulifrons, from Obi-Major, is similar, except that it has a large, yellow frontal caruncle.

P. geelvinkiana, from the islands in Geelvink Bay, is green, with a gray cap, chin, and spots on the wings; throat and breast crimson.

The ORANGE-BELLIED FRUIT DOVE *(P. iozonus),* from New Guinea and nearby islands, is emerald green, with a large orange patch on the belly; its vent is yellow. It has been imported.

P. insolitus from the Bismarck Archipelago, resembles *iozonus,* but it has a large, yellow frontal caruncle, and gray wing patches.

The DWARF FRUIT DOVE *(P. naina),* from the Western Papuan Islands and Southern New Guinea, is green, with yellow on the wings and vent, and a small violet patch on the belly. This fruit dove is tiny.

WALLACE'S FRUIT DOVE *(P. wallacei),* from the Aru and nearby islands, is fairly large. It has been imported frequently. Its plumage is gaudy: crimson crown; white throat; neck, breast, and upper-back gray; a white crescent on the breast is followed by an orange patch; the vent is yellow; and the remainder of the plumage is green, the wings having gray patches.

The ORANGE-FRONTED FRUIT DOVE *(P. aurantiifrons),* from New Guinea and vicinity, is green with gray spots above; the forehead orange; chin and throat white; neck and upper-breast ashy-gray; upper-back gray and orange; the vent yellowish-white.

The ORNATE FRUIT DOVE (*P. ornatus*) and its subspecies *gestroi*, which also has been imported, are green, with a red or golden cap, gray nape and cheeks, and a yellow-gray throat; upper-back and upper-breast yellowish-red; the center of the belly and the vent are yellowish-white; scapulars are gray and orange; the tail is tipped with yellow. This rather large bird has been imported occasionally.

The SPOTTED FRUIT DOVE (*P. perlatus*) is quite similar: dark-green above, its wings spotted with pink. It also comes from New Guinea and vicinity.

P. tannensis, from the New Hebrides and Banks Islands, is also more or less similar, but has yellow wing patches.

Three remarkable, small species of *Ptilinopus*, often separated as *Chrysoena*, inhabit the Fiji Islands. The females are all similar: dark green with yellowish heads. The males are strikingly different, having velvety or pointed feathers.

The VELVET FRUIT DOVE (*P. layardi*), from the Kandavu group, is dark-green, with a greenish-yellow head.

The ORANGE FRUIT DOVE (*P. victor*), from Vanna Levu, Tavuini, and neighboring islands, is a beautiful reddish-orange, with an olive-yellow head—one of the finest doves extant.

The GOLDEN DOVE (*P. luteovirens*) has hackle-shaped breast, back and wing feathers, and is colored golden olive-yellow; its belly and vent are light yellow. It is found on Viti Levu and nearby islands.

Two very peculiar species live in the Philippines, resembling Fruit Doves in habit and shape but Seed-Eating doves in color and pattern.

The WHITE-EARED BROWN FRUIT DOVE (*Phapitreron leucotis*) is brown, bronzy on the upper-parts; its crown is gray; nape and hind-neck bronze-green; a black line runs below the eyes, and a white or creamy one underneath; the face and breast are fulvous. The sexes are similarly colored. A few of the several races have found their way into captivity.

The AMETHYST BROWN FRUIT DOVE (*P. amethystina*) is larger, with a much stronger and longer bill; otherwise, it is very similar, except for cinnamon instead of gray under tail-coverts, and a violet, not green, nuchal collar. Both species, found throughout the islands, are at present in Mr. Strann's collection.

BLUE WART PIGEONS

A very special, though small, group of Fruit Pigeons inhabit Madagascar and the neighboring islands of Aldabra, the Comoros, and the Seychelles. Another one, now extinct, lived on Mauritius. These pigeons are very dark blue and have bright, vermilion-red wattles between the beak and the eyes. They are of moderate size, with square and fairly short tails. The sexes are alike. In captivity, they thrive on the usual Fruit Dove diet, but they are very seldom available.

The RED-CROWNED WART PIGEON *(Alectroenas pulcherima)*, from the Seychelles Islands, is deep blue, with head, neck, upper-back and upper-breast pearl gray, the feathers being pointed; the crown is crimson. This handsome species was bred in my outdoor aviaries at Villers-Bretonneux between 1914 and 1918, where it fed on boiled potatoes, rice, crushed hemp, and various fruit. Since these pigeons are not hardy, they must be kept indoors during cold winters. My birds proved so quarrelsome that pairs had to be isolated. The young are barred dark greenish-gray and yellow.

SGANZIN'S WART PIGEON *(A. sganzini)*, from the Comoros and Aldabra, is deep blue-black, with head, neck, upper-back, and upper-breast dark gray.

The MADAGASCAR WART PIGEON *(A. madagascariensis)* is dark blue; neck and throat gray; tail and coverts dark crimson. Cleres received a specimen in 1929.

GREEN FRUIT PIGEONS

Green pigeons inhabit Africa, southern Asia, the Philippines, Japan, Celebes, and Malaysia, south to the Lesser Sunda Islands and Buru. Except for the male of one Malaysian species, all are mainly pale yellowish-green, the black flight feathers bordered yellow. They live mostly in flocks on trees, where they feed on fruit. Perching motionless and silently, they hold their bodies almost horizontal, and are for this reason hard to detect. They have the curious habit of running up branches. All have crimson legs and feet, except two species in which they are yellow, and another one in which they are orange. Usually they have some blue, bare skin around eyes and beak, and their iris shows blue and

Red-crowned Wart Pigeon *(Alectroenas pulcherrima).*

pink, or orange circles. Often the base of the bill is red. Green Fruit Pigeons are occasionally imported, but frequently they arrive with soiled plumage and in otherwise poor condition. When they are clean and healthy, they do well in confinement and will breed. Their flute-like cooing is very pleasant in some species, but in others it is harsh.

Green Fruit Pigeons of the genus *Sphenurus* have long, graduated, sometimes pointed tails. They are large birds. Owing to their melodious coo, they are prized as cagebirds in their native countries—from India to Japan, the northern Philippines and Malaysia. They flock less than the other species.

The INDIAN PINTAIL GREEN PIGEON *(S. apicauda)*, indigenous from the Himalayas to Tonkin and Annam, has a long, pointed tail. Its color is yellowish-green, the hind-neck washed gray, and the breast tinged orange; vent and under tail-coverts are cinnamon; the tail is gray and black. This very beautiful pigeon is rarely imported.

The WHITE-BELLIED PINTAIL GREEN PIGEON *(S. seimundi)*, from the mountains of Malaya and South Annam, is dark apple green, with a gray wash on its upper back, and orange tinge on the breast, and small, vinaceous-red shoulder patches; the center of the belly is white, the tail black; the under tail-coverts yellow. The hen has neither red patches nor orange tinge. A rare, but rather dull-colored pigeon.

The YELLOW-BELLIED PINTAIL GREEN PIGEON *(S. oxyurus)* resembles *seimundi*, but has no shoulder patches. Its belly is yellow; tail less pointed and greenish; under tail-coverts are light-cinnamon; the wings without yellow borders. This pigeon lives in the hills of Sumatra and Java.

The WEDGE-TAILED GREEN PIGEON *(S. sphenurus)* inhabits the mountains of northern India, from Kashmir to Assam, Burma, Siam, Indochina, Yunnan, Hainan and Malaysia, as far east as Lombok, and it has many local races. Its coloring is yellowish-green, the breast tinged with orange, the upper-parts washed gray; the tail is not pointed, but graduated and broad, and grayish-green; on the shoulders is a large vinous patch. The hen is green all over. This widespread species, with an euphonious coo, is often found in aviaries. In England, the late Mr. Shore-Bailey bred it. In India, it is a favorite cage-bird.

The JAPANESE GREEN PIGEON *(S. sieboldi)* is large, yellowish-green, with a white belly; its shoulders are vinous; its forehead and throat yellow. Often kept as a "songbird," a subspecies *(sororius)* is also found in Formosa.

The FORMOSAN GREEN PIGEON *(S. formosae)*, whose habitat extends to the Ryukyu Islands and the northern Philippines, is green, with pinkish-maroon shoulders. The male has an ochraceous cap.

All other Green Pigeons have shorter, square tails and belong to the genus *Treron*. Large flocks of them live together, and their voice, which varies, is usually loud. One of these species is large;

another one, very small. All others are of medium size.

The LARGE GREEN PIGEON *(T. capellei)* is the giant of the genus. It has a thick, curved beak. The male's coloring is light green, with an orange breast; ashy-black flight feathers, margined with yellow; a green and gray tail, and a dark chestnut under-tail. The hen has a yellowish upper-head and a pale, grayish-cinnamon under-tail. This pigeon, common in the Malayasian forests, is occasionally imported, but is too coarse to be attractive.

The THICK-BILLED GREEN PIGEON *(T. curvirostra)* is represented by numerous local varieties spread from Nepal to Indochina, Hainan, Malaysia, and the northeastern Philippines. Of medium size, this pigeon has a thick, curved bill, whose horny plate reaches the forehead. Predominantly apple-green, the male's crown is gray, his mantle maroon-red with an ochraceous breast tinge, which the hen lacks. This pigeon, common at low altitudes, is fairly often found in aviaries.

The POMPADOUR GREEN PIGEON *(T. pompadora)* is indigenous to India and Ceylon, east to Cochin China, the Philippines, Malaysia, Celebes, and the Lesser Sunda Islands. The most widespread of all Asiatic Green Pigeons, its geographic races vary considerably. Though resembling *curvirostra*, it is larger; its bill is smaller, and more gray appears on its head. Now and then it gets into fanciers' hands.

The CINNAMON-HEADED GREEN PIGEON *(T. fulvicollis)* is a rather rare, low-country species from Malaya, Sumatra, Borneo, and nearby islands, where it frequents mangroves. The male's head and mantle are rusty-cinnamon, turning vinous on the back; rump and tail are dark green, showing some yellow on the thighs; the under tail-coverts are cinnamon. The hen is green, washed above with gray; her crown also is gray, whereas the vent, thighs, and under-tail appear buffy-white, spotted with dark green.

The LITTLE GREEN PIGEON *(T. olax)*, the group's pigmy, quite rare in Malaysia, is found in the dense forests at low and moderately high elevations. The male's plumage is colored as follows: head, neck, and upper-back green; middle back and wing-coverts maroon-red; rump and tail dark gray; breast ochraceous-orange; under-parts green; and under tail-coverts cinnamon. The female is dull grayish-green.

The PINK-NECKED GREEN PIGEON *(T. vernans)*, ranges from Tenessarim and southern Indochina to Malaysia, the Philippines, and Celebes. The head of the male is bluish-gray; his neck and upper-breast are powdery lilac-pink; his lower breast is orange; his belly yellowish-green; his under-tail coverts cinnamon; his tail gray; his upper-parts pale green; his wings are black with a yellow border. The female is pale grayish-green and has a gray tail. This very pretty pigeon is fairly frequently seen in captivity.

The ORANGE-BREASTED GREEN PIGEON *(T. bicincta)* resembles *vernans* but is larger. In the male, the head and tail are bright green; nape and neck gray. The species is common throughout India, Ceylon, Indochina, Hainan, Malaya and Java.

The YELLOW-LEGGED GREEN PIGEON *(T. phoenicoptera)*, indigenous to India, Ceylon, Burma, Siam, and southern Indochina, is more like the African species than its Asiatic relatives. It is a rather large, fairly long-tailed pigeon—the only one of its kind in Asia with yellow legs. Cock and hen are alike. This pigeon's head is green and gray; the hind-neck chrome-yellow and gray; the upper-parts yellowish olive-green; the tail gray, with a yellow base; there is a lilac-vinous patch on the shoulders; the flights are bordered yellow; the breast is yellow; the flanks and belly are gray; yellow patches appearing on vent and thighs; the under tail-coverts are chestnut. This pleasant-voiced pigeon is fairly often imported.

Four species of Green Pigeons are found in Africa and another one in Madagascar.

The MADAGASCAR GREEN PIGEON *(T. australis)* has a yellowish-green head, neck, and breast; olive-green upper-parts, washed with gray; wings with a vinous shoulder patch and a pale yellow band on the coverts; tail and sides gray. The flanks are dark olive; the under-tail cinnamon and white. Its bill is thin.

The SAO THOME GREEN PIGEON *(T. s. thomae)* has a short thick bill; head, neck, and breast greenish-gray; upper-parts dark olive; a dark purple shoulder patch and a pale yellow band on the wing-coverts; the tail is gray; the belly yellow. The London Zoo has kept this species.

The YELLOW-BELLIED GREEN PIGEON *(T. waalia)* occurs in West Africa, east to Kenya, Somaliland, Eritrea, southern Arabia, and Socotra Island. Except for its red legs, it closely resembles the Asiatic *phoenicoptera*. Head, neck, and upper breast are gray; the lower breast is yellow; upper-parts olive-green, with a vinous shoulder patch; the black flights are bordered with yellow; the tail is black and gray. It is fairly often kept in captivity.

DELALANDE'S GREEN PIGEON *(T. delalandei)*, from South and East Africa, is light green, with gray nape, vinous shoulder patches and yellow thighs. Its legs are orange. It is occasionally imported.

The BARE-FACED GREEN PIGEON *(T. calva)*, true to its name, has a bald, bulging forehead. It is found throughout Africa, except the North, and it has many local races. Its head and neck are yellowish olive-green, shading to gray on the mantle; the remaining upper-parts are dark olive; there is a vinous shoulder patch and the blackish flights are yellow-margined; the wing-coverts are yellow-barred; under-parts green; the under-tail is creamy and cinnamon. The legs are yellow. This, the commonest of African Green Pigeons, is frequently imported, but usually in poor condition.

INDEX

Page numbers printed in *italic* face refer to photographs.